KAY ZIMMERMAN

Rebuilding the HOUSE OF THE LORD

PREPARATION FOR GOD'S GLORY

Copyright © 2018 by Kay Zimmerman.

All rights reserved. No part of this publication may be reproduced, distributed, or transmitted in any form or by any means, including photocopying, recording, or other electronic or mechanical methods, without the prior written permission of the author, except in the case of brief quotations embodied in critical reviews and certain other noncommercial uses permitted by copyright law.

Unless otherwise indicated, Bible quotations are taken from the New Spirit-Filled Life Bible version of the Bible. Copyright (c) 2002 by Thomas Nelson Bibles, a Division of Thomas Nelson, Inc.

All other quotes are from The Amplified Bible Expanded Edition. Copyright (c) 1987 by Zondervan Bible Publishers by the Zondervan Corporation.

Definitions from: Merriam-Webster's Collegiate Dictionary. Copyright (c) 1997 by Merriam-Webster, Incorporated.

An Expository Dictionary of New Testament Words by W.E.Vine. Published by Fleming H. Revell Company. (I see no copyright information)

All songs and poetry originated from the author, Kay Zimmerman, as the Lord ministered them to her.

Printed in the United States of America

ISBN: 978-1-949362-15-2 *(Paperback)*
ISBN: 978-1-949362-16-9 *(Hardback)*
ISBN: 978-1-949362-14-5 *(eBook)*

Library of Congress Control Number: 2018952047

 STONEWALL PRESS
PAVING YOUR WAY TO SUCCESS

Stonewall Press
363 Paladium Court
Owings Mills, MD 21117
www.stonewallpress.com
1-888-334-0980

"Kay Zimmerman is a gifted woman of God whom we have known for over twenty years. As a pastor and as a conference speaker, she has an anointing to impart faith, freedom, and the fire of God. She has been ordained under our Dunamis ministry as a Minister of the Gospel of Jesus Christ. Kay has traveled with us in ministry to several nations including Peru, Brazil, France, and here in the United States, and we have seen the good fruit of her ministry. We can attest that she is a woman of integrity and anointing."

Dennis and Lynnie Walker
Directors: Dunamis ARC

"Pastor Kay is a blessing for our entire community, but especially for our City workers to whom she gives extra special attention through focused prayer and positive reinforcement. In what sometimes feels like a critical, thankless world, Pastor Kay provides a continuous ray of sunshine that we can always count on. Thank you, Pastor Kay. We truly appreciate you and everything you hold true."

Charlie Cassens
City Manager
Lake Havasu City, Arizona

"We have known Kay Zimmerman for many years and have had the opportunity on many occasions to minister together. In the over forty years she has walked with the Lord, she has been a great blessing to thousands to whom she has had the opportunity to minister. She is like a breath of fresh air that comes like 'A rushing mighty wind' with the revelation and empowerment of the Spirit of God everywhere she goes. God has used her in an awesome way to bring a spirit of unity to the body of Christ in numerous regions."

Dr. A. L. & Joyce Gill
Gill Ministries
Big Bear Lake, California

"Rebuilding the House of the Lord is a great read for everyone. It is very well written. When God comes into our lives He wants to help us become a better version, the best version, of who we are capable of becoming. In this book, Kay Zimmerman does an excellent job giving us stories from the Bible and from her life to see how God rebuilds us."

Greg Brown
Leader of Skyway Church and
ASCEND International Network
Goodyear, AZ

"As a student of Gateway International Bible Institute in Phoenix, Arizona, our assignment was to read Kay Zimmerman's book, Rebuilding the House of the Lord.

What a joy it was to read this book as it was written with much wisdom. Thank you Pastor Kay for being so real! You are God's handwork and a true servant in bringing God's love clearer to His people. Loved your book! I want to reread it!"

Pastor June Esposito
Glendale, AZ

"Apostle Kay's book easily adapts scriptures to various situations. I enjoyed reading it because it was down to earth, humorous, and sincere."

Irma Chavez
Waddell, AZ

Contents

ACKNOWLEDGEMENTS vii

CHAPTER ONE	IT'S TIME TO REBUILD!...................	1
CHAPTER TWO	HE CARES ABOUT THE ONE........	9
CHAPTER THREE	THE CALL...	17
CHAPTER FOUR	THE POWER WEAPON	29
CHAPTER FIVE	PREPARATION FOR GREATNESS	41
CHAPTER SIX	GRUMBLIN' IN THE WILDERNESS OR ENJOYING THE JOURNEY?...	63
CHAPTER SEVEN	DYING TO LIVE...............................	79
CHAPTER EIGHT	ONENESS..	89
CHAPTER NINE	KINGDOM MINDSET	103
CHAPTER TEN	AXING THE ROOTS	115
CHAPTER ELEVEN	DEVELOPING LISTENING SKILLS...............................	121
CHAPTER TWELVE	BATHING IN GOD'S LOVE	127
CHAPTER THIRTEEN	VISITING CAMP COMPARISON	135
CHAPTER FOURTEEN	DON'T BITE THE BAIT	139
CHAPTER FIFTEEN	DANCING UPON INJUSTICE	143
CHAPTER SIXTEEN	FRESH BREAD	155
CHAPTER SEVENTEEN	RAGS TO RICHES.........................	161
CHAPTER EIGHTEEN	TENACITY (STICKING TO IT)...	169
CHAPTER NINETEEN	FIGHT THE GOOD FIGHT.........	179
CHAPTER TWENTY	LIGHTING THE WAY....................	185
CHAPTER TWENTY-ONE	SEEING HIS GLORY	193

ACKNOWLEDGEMENTS

Many thanks to my grandson Alex for inspiring me to start this book. It has taken some twists and turns since that day we had lunch together at Golden Corral. However, I received the chapter titles that same night, but the title of the book has changed.

Thanks also to my husband Jerry for his patience with me as he lovingly kept prodding me to get this book finished.

Thanks to my friend Kathi Livingston for her honesty in advising me that I needed to adjust the presentation. Though I groaned inside at the idea of added work to complete it, it wasn't as difficult as I thought and I'm grateful for the advice.

Thank you to my friend Bea Evans, who has always believed in me and encouraged me to keep focused and move forward.

Thanks also to those who helped me to learn these life lessons, whether knowingly or unknowingly.

Thank you, awesome God, for your love and encouragement and for being in the center of my life!

CHAPTER ONE

IT'S TIME TO REBUILD!

Have you been hanging out in that old, worn-out, broken-down house that always needs fixing, where there are cracks and dents in the walls, maybe even holes? It's where you often hear the sound of creaking and moaning and groaning, like blame, guilt, condemnation, fear, doubt, and unbelief. It's where the carpet you walk on is worn and stained, and where you feel tired and discouraged, possibly even fearful and hopeless. It feels stuffy and confining and there may be cobwebs hanging from the ceiling.

As you breathe in, you almost choke, as you smell stale mildew and mold, and it seems like everything you touch in this house has a film of dust. As you look around, everything seems to be in disarray and disorder and you feel overwhelmed, as you seem to have lost control, lost ambition, lost heart, and certainly lost vision.

Do you feel stuck and boxed-in where you are, even paralyzed? Why in the world would you linger there in that dark dreary place?

Take heart! A provision for a new house has been made for you! When you invite Jesus to live in your heart, He invites you to step out of the old house and into the new one, created in Christ Jesus!

God has provided for you a brand new house! There's nothing broken or worn out or dilapidated in this house. It's a glorious house! The vivid colors of the fresh paint are literally out of this world! Everything is bright and shining! It's a beautiful house! It's just heavenly!

There are treasures in this house of gold and silver, of ruby and emerald, sapphire, and every kind of beautiful gem imaginable! It's all sparkling and glorious!

The sound system in the new house releases the sound of heaven that shakes the earth and transforms the atmosphere! Light and life pulsate throughout your being!

When you step into this house and take a deep breath, it smells clean and fresh and exhilarating! It smells heavenly!

Oh! The sensations I feel when I step into my new house! I am energized and faith arises in my spirit, love saturates my heart, and hope stirs up my mind!

As I was writing this allegory, several scriptures about "my house" came to mind that aligned with it.

> *And if it seems evil to you to serve the Lord, choose for yourselves this day whom you will serve, whether the gods which your fathers served that were on the other side of the River, or the gods of the Amorites, in whose land you dwell. But as for me and my house, we will serve the Lord.* (Joshua 24:15)

Amorites (highlanders) are one of the nations of Canaan before the Hebrew conquest. They were on both sides of the Jordan River, dwelling in the mountains. I feel strongly impressed that the Amorites represent pride. Believers and unbelievers alike may stay stuck where they are rather than admit they need help. That's pride! We are to jump into the

River of God and get saturated with that living water until it overflows the riverbanks, overtakes our foolish pride, and drowns our enemies that stand against and try to prohibit the plans and purposes of God.

> *And I said to you, "You have come to the mountains of the Amorites, which the Lord our God is giving us. Look, the Lord your God has set the land before you; go up and possess it, as the Lord God of your fathers has spoken to you, do not fear or be discouraged." .... Then I said to you, "Do not be terrified, or afraid of them. The Lord your God, who goes before you, He will fight for you, according to all He did for you in Egypt before your eyes."* (Deuteronomy 1:21, 29, & 30)

God has given you a new house. That new house is already yours. You just need to step into it and begin to possess it. Are you afraid to move from where you are, in your comfort zone? Don't be afraid. To the same degree God did miracles for the Israelites in Egypt, He'll do miracles for you!

> *Therefore, if anyone is in Christ, he is a new creation, old things have passed away; behold, all things have become new.* (II Corinthians 5:17)

> *Through wisdom a house is built, and by understanding it is established; by knowledge the rooms are filled with all precious and pleasant riches.* (Proverbs 24:3,4)

Jesus is our wisdom. By knowing Him and pressing in to Him, listening to Him and enjoying His presence, as well as by studying God's Word, and spending time with people of faith, we receive the wisdom of God and understanding of His ways. There is greater wisdom released when in that corporate anointing with other believers.

> Jesus said, *"Every kingdom divided against itself is brought to desolation, and every city or house divided against itself will not stand."* (Matthew 12:25)

Everything in the house needs to come into alignment with the kingdom of God. My mind, my tongue, my emotions, my character, and my actions need to be saturated with the Spirit of God and come into alignment with God's kingdom and God's purpose.

> *Put off, concerning your former conduct, the old man which grows corrupt according to the deceitful lusts, and be renewed in the spirit of your mind, and put on the new man which was created according to God, in true righteousness and holiness.* (Ephesians 4:22-24)

Some say Christianity is a "put on." It's true. Put off the old sinful man. Get out of that house. Put on the brand new one created according to God. Step on into that new one!

> *For every house is built by someone, but He who built all things is God. Christ is a Son over His own house, whose house we are if we hold fast the confidence and the rejoicing of the hope firm to the end.* (Hebrews 3:4,6)

Holding fast to continual confidence and rejoicing qualifies us to be His house, according to this verse. Tough times and difficult circumstances tend to wear down your confidence and deplete you of joy. That's why we need to hold fast and firm to faith and joy so they are continual components in our life, if this new house we live in belongs totally to Jesus.

> *For we are God's fellow workers; you are God's field, you are God's building. Do you not know that you are the*

temple of God and that the Spirit of God dwells in you? (I Corinthians 3:9,16)

God is the Builder. We are the building. This is a process. We must allow Him room to build and allow Him to use whatever tools He chooses. Usually the tools He uses are people or objects we would not have chosen. Our part is to surrender to the Builder and say, "Build on, God!"

> *Therefore we were buried with Him through baptism and death, that just as Christ was raised from the dead by the glory of the Father, even so we also should walk in newness of life. For if we have been united together in the likeness of His death, certainly we also shall be in the likeness of His resurrection.* (Romans 6:4,5)

Jesus identified with us and our sin when He went to the cross. He actually became our sin and it was nailed to the cross, put to death once for all! We were united with Him, one with Him. We need to identify with Him on the cross, buried in the tomb, and visualize ourselves coming forth from the tomb in resurrection power!

> *We were buried with Jesus in baptism, in which you also were raised with Him through faith in the working of God, who raised Him from the dead. We were dead in our trespasses and He made us alive together with Him, having forgiven us all trespasses.* (Ephesians 2:12,13)

> *But God, who is rich in mercy, because of His great love with which He loved us, even when we were dead in trespasses, made us alive together with Christ (by grace you have been saved), and raised us up together, and made us sit together in the heavenly places in Christ Jesus.* (Ephesians 2:4-6)

Does that not grip your heart? I remember when I was dead in trespasses. I did much more to hinder the kingdom of God than I did to promote it. In the midst of that, God showed me His mercy! He loved me with His great love, and reached down to me and brought me up to sit in heavenly places! That's where I am spiritually, according to God's Word. I am in the process, mentally, emotionally, and in my experience, of being transformed to this position so I can have a heavenly perspective.

It is time to take your assigned seat! Where? Sitting together in the heavenly places in Christ! That's the best seat in the house, don't you think? We need to get that picture in our minds and meditate upon it until it becomes a reality! From that seat, the view is entirely different! We see through God's perspective, where there is always hope, always love, and always the promise of a better future!

From your assigned seat in heaven, you will begin to see more clearly your assignment on this earth.

Since about 1980, I have heard the Lord speak to me many times saying, "Rebuild the house of the Lord." I had no clue what He was talking about back then, except that I knew it had to do with my assignment. Since then I've spent many years ministering to individuals and helping them to rebuild their house, by helping them to remove strongholds of the enemy, helping them to be set free of the effects, and helping them to rebuild their lives based on the truth.

For many years, I've been involved with rebuilding the church (body of believers), helping them to remove wrong teachings and traditions, tearing down those belief systems that are in opposition to plans and purposes of God; thereby helping to rebuild the body of Christ.

I've also been leading a group of pastors for many years, who are seeking God together for His vision and direction for our city. We are asking Him to expose those things that divide us and to set us free from them, allowing God to bring us into such oneness that the world will know that God sent Jesus and loves them just as He loves Jesus!

The longer I've known My Father God, the more I've seen He is into multitasking. While He's working with individuals, it's not just all about me! He's also working with the church and He's working in the city. He really only sees one church in each city according to how He addressed the church in Revelations.

This book contains many of life's lessons that have been valuable to me. I've been walking with God wholeheartedly for over forty years and I have much more to learn of Him. However, He has taught me some very valuable lessons along the way. I believe God wants me to share them with others, so I open my heart and my life to you and welcome you. Enjoy the journey with me as we are rebuilt together.

The following is a very healthy exercise to get you started.

REBUILD THE HOUSE OF THE LORD

1. Please close your eyes.
2. Focus on heaven.
3. Take your assigned seat.
4. Ask Jesus to come and show you your house.
5. Linger there while He shows you. Do not be in a hurry. He is faithful to come to those who wait.
6. Ask Him to reveal to you what needs to be removed.
7. Reach in and remove those things that hinder you, keep you from your destiny, and cause you pain and discomfort along the way.
8. Lift them up and give them to Jesus. Watch Him remove them and shatter them.
9. Ask Holy Spirit to fill every empty space. Just receive.

CHAPTER TWO

HE CARES ABOUT THE ONE

It's amazing to me how much Jesus cares for each individual house. He treasures each one and pays great attention to details. The story of the Samaritan woman demonstrates that. I believe it was the first story from the Bible that I really heard. My sister-in-law Faye had invited me that Sunday morning to the little white United Methodist Church in Deckerville, Michigan. Reverend Weeks was telling the story of a woman who had been rejected, whose life was all messed up. Yet Jesus came to her and poured love into her, and her life was totally changed!

I immediately related to that woman, and instantly I had hope for my life! I didn't give Jesus my life that day, as I didn't even know how, but the seed of hope was planted. As I reflect on how intricately God worked out details in my life to bring me to the point of surrender, I am even now amazed! At the end of that service, Reverend Weeks announced they were going to have a counseling class beginning that Wednesday. I had often thought I would like to be a counselor for young people, because I had desperately needed help as a kid and there had been no one to help me. I signed up for the class. When I attended the class on Wednesday night, I discovered that Reverend Weeks was teaching the salvation scriptures to prepare people to counsel at the altar for the upcoming revival in April. I had absolutely no understanding of what a revival was and I had never even read a Bible before, but I found my dad's old Bible and began to memorize those scriptures.

My sister and I were taking a Dale Carnegie Course at the time and it was causing me to stop and reflect on my life, as we had to give speeches about many different personal experiences.

By the time the revival began on April 6th, I was ready. I walked into that church and looked around. I saw people I had known as a young person who had been pretty rough. They were now aglow with the Spirit of the Lord! They began to give testimonies as to how Jesus had totally changed them! Then the evangelist, Mahlon Felkins, walked in. I had never seen or heard anyone so full of the love of God! It just radiated through him to everyone! He told of how he had been very mean all of his life and had been in prison for attempted murder. In prison someone brought him a Bible and he had cursed and thrown it on the floor; yet later that night, he picked it up and began to read it. He repented that night and turned his life over to Jesus! He was instantly transformed by the power of God!

When Mahlon gave the invitation to accept Christ that night, I was the first one to run to the altar. I fell on my knees and cried out, "Lord, just take all that I am and all that I have. Give me all that You are and all that You have!" Instantly I was transformed! I saw with new eyes! I heard with new ears! During that revival, one hundred people in Deckerville came to the Lord. The population of that town was only eight hundred! There were so many at the altar, I turned around and began leading others to the Lord the same night I was saved! I began walking in miracle power! You can read about those miracles in my first book, God Stories. From the moment I was born again, it has been my greatest desire to introduce others to Jesus and see them transformed.

Let's take a look at the story of the Samaritan woman. The Samaritans were a hated and rejected people. Why? People of God had lived there, but they secretly did things against the Lord. They rejected God and became idol worshipers, like the nations around them. They become so wicked that, after warning them many times and they refused to hear, God removed them out of His sight, from their own land. (11 Kings 17:23)

The king of Assyria brought people from Babylon, Cuthah, Ava, Hamath, and Sepharvaim, and other places, and placed them in Samaria in place of the children of Israel. These foreigners took possession of it. They were idol worshipers and they were so wicked that the Lord sent lions among them, which killed some of them. The people complained that they didn't even know the rituals of the God of the land, so the king sent priests to come back and teach them. However, they all still continued to make gods of their own, and put them in shrines in high places. They even burned their own children. They served their own gods and continued practicing their own ungodly rituals. God's people were not to mix with these people.

Jesus had told his disciples not to go to Samaria. Yet one day Jesus was departing from Judea & going to Galilee. He said *He needed to go through Samaria.* (John 4:4)

I love how Jesus is all about the one. His eye is on the one who is hungering and thirsting. He knew there was a woman there who would respond to Him.

Many times in my life, God moved in situations to place me with someone who desperately needed a touch from Him. One time, when I was on my way to China, He allowed my plane to be late in Las Vegas so I would miss my connecting flight, in order for me to have breakfast in San Francisco with a Muslim woman and lead her to Jesus.

A few weeks later, by my own error, we missed a flight in Las Vegas and had to be rerouted through Phoenix, having to purchase new tickets. We were waiting quite some time at the gate when I asked the Lord where my divine appointment was. He highlighted to me a blond lady, sitting across from me. I began to ask her questions and soon I was ministering inner healing and deliverance to a very needy Christian lady, who was set free of anxiety and depression! Jesus is all about the one!

Jesus arrived in Samaria at the well about noon. Though He was hot and weary and thirsty from His journey, He waited for that certain woman.

The woman of Samaria arrived at the well. She was the only one, because most people wouldn't come in the heat of day to draw water. More than likely, she came at that time to avoid the rejection, as she was not only a Samaritan, she had a terrible reputation in the community because of her lifestyle.

It didn't stop Jesus. To her amazement, He asked her for a drink.

> *She asked Him, "Why would You, a Jew, ask me, a Samaritan woman, for a drink. Jews don't have any dealings with Samaritans." (John 4:12)*

> *Jesus answered her, "Whoever drinks of this water will thirst again, but whoever drinks of the water that I will give him will never thirst. But the water that I shall give him will become in him a fountain of water springing up into everlasting life." (John 4:13,14)*

The word drinks is not a one-time action. It is a continual drinking. The fountain of water is the living water of the Holy

Spirit. The invitation is to "whoever". That includes all of us who will continue to drink in of the Holy Spirit. He'll satisfy every thirst!

This nameless woman responded exactly the way each one of us should.

"Give me this water." (John 4:15)

Jesus said to her, "Go, call your husband, and come here." (John 4:16)

Jesus knew she had no husband. He wanted her to tell Him that, which she did. He continued,

"You have well said, 'I have no husband', for you have had five husbands, and the one whom you now have is not your husband; in that you spoke truly." (John 4:17,18)

Jesus is so amazing! He pressed beyond the cultural beliefs! He pressed beyond the religion! He pressed beyond the fact that she was a woman! He wasn't concerned about His reputation as He encountered her by Himself. Her reputation and her lifestyle didn't stop Him! His love was more powerful and compelling than all that!

Jesus knew so much about her that she recognized He was a prophet. Then she quickly changed the subject, turning it from her lifestyle.

She brought up the subject of worship, and Jesus told her:

"True worshipers will worship the Father in spirit and truth; for the Father is seeking such to worship Him. God is Spirit, and those who worship Him must worship in spirit and truth." (John 14:23,24)

The Father is actually seeking people who will worship honestly and freely before Him, led by the Holy Spirit. He desires that we know Him in truth, not just based upon our own experience, but upon Who He says He is. He wants us to be real with Him. Be honest and transparent before Him. Our worship develops out of our relationship with Him, based on trust in Him and faith in Him.

She then brought up the Messiah, and Jesus said to her,

"I who speak to you am He." (John 4:26)

When His disciples showed up, they marveled that He was talking to a woman, as Jews considered it improper for a rabbi to speak to a woman in public. Yet Jesus had treated her with respect, a very important key. If we are going to gain an opening with people, no matter who they are or where they have been, we need to show them respect, as Jesus does.

That woman left her water pot, went into the city and said to the men,

"Come, see a Man who told me all things that I ever did. Could this be the Christ?" (John 4:29)

In this, she was a wise lady. Instead of telling these men flat out that this was the Christ, she did as Jesus often did, and asked them a question. She peaked their curiosity. It worked. They came to Jesus.

The disciples arrived with the food and they felt Jesus should stop what He was doing and eat. He responded,

"My food is to do the will of Him who sent Me, and to finish His work." (John 4:34)

He was saying that He is nourished as He is doing what the Father is asking Him to do. So it is with us. We need to turn our attention from our own needs and catch the initiatives of the Father. As we do what we see the Father doing, we will receive nourishment and strength. He continued talking about the harvest. The heart of the Father is upon bringing people into relationship with Him. That's His will and the work He has given us to do. I'm not talking about just being busy. I'm talking about hearing what the Father is saying, and doing exactly that. Again I hear the words the Father spoke to me years ago in a dream, "Do only what God has told you to do."

> *Many of the Samaritans of that city believed in Him because of the word of the woman who testified, "He told me all that I ever did."* (John 4:39)

Have you thought of all the barriers this woman had to press through in order to run out into the city and tell the men what had happened to her? She had to press through the rejection of being a Samaritan. She had to press through the rejection of being a woman. She had to press through the rejection of being divorced five times. She had to press through the barrier of her bad reputation for living with a man unmarried.

No matter where you have come from or what you have done, many will come to the Lord as we testify of what He has done for us!

Those Samaritans talked Jesus into staying for two days, *and many more believed in Him because of His word.* (John 4:41)

That woman of Samaria, whose name we don't even know, impacted a whole city! She was a great evangelist! What an example to us! We can press through any obstacle, any rejection, and do the work the Father has called us to, in order to impact our city, our region, our state, our nation, or whatever nation to which God calls us!

We are all called to be evangelists. Don't look back at where you've been or what you've done. Look forward to Jesus and wherever He is calling you to go!

CHAPTER THREE

THE CALL

What is your house designed and created to be? Many struggle with this question. "What am I even here for? What is my life all about?" Only the Designer, our Heavenly Father, has those answers. Every detail and feature was intricately designed for a purpose. He desires that we seek Him, and He delights in revealing the purpose to us.

So, as we seek Him, the clouds part and the heavens are opened. A bolt of lightning hits the ground directly in front of you. An extremely loud booming voice comes from heaven declaring, "Kay, you are called to start a ministry!"

Ok, so maybe not. Probably not. Almost never! But there's a still, small voice inside of you or an impression that keeps coming upon you that indicates that's exactly what God wants you to do. There's also a desire in your heart to do it.

Delight yourself in the Lord, and He shall give you the desires of your heart. (Psalm 37:5)

Oftentimes you have a desire in your heart and you try to make it go away because you think it's just your own fleshly desire. The key is: When do you sense that desire? Is it when you are delighting yourself in the Lord?

An effective way to pray at a time like that is, "Lord, if this desire is coming from You, please increase that desire in me. If it is not from You, please take it from my heart." Spend time praising Him, which invokes His presence. Then spend time soaking in His presence and listening to Him.

If it is God, He will continue to confirm it to you. He won't just tell you once and if you don't get it the first time, you're disqualified. God is very patient and kind.

While you're waiting, two major attacks will normally come. The first attack is usually from your own mind. It's called, "Who am I?"

I remember vividly the night I asked Jesus to come into my heart and take over my life, when I was overwhelmed with His love and power! In an instant my heart changed and I was filled with His Holy Spirit! I didn't even know what that was, but all I wanted to do, from that moment on, was to help others to also have an encounter with Him so they could experience His peace, love and joy! I began devouring the Word of God, and walking in miracle power. Nothing else really satisfied me like sharing Jesus with others. It was my passion to minister to people! Though I immediately began leading others to Jesus, I never even considered that God would want me to be a pastor.

I was asked a few weeks later to teach a Sunday School class for little children, and I accepted. I really had to study then, because I didn't know one Bible story. I was learning so much more than the children, and I loved it. The next year, I was asked to speak the first night of the revival. I was shocked, honored, and thrilled, but a little scared. Soon I was asked to be the Teen Leader and I accepted.

Though I had such a burning desire to minister to people, I kept thinking of all the reasons why I couldn't be a pastor, and I made excuses for not doing it. First of all, I was a woman. Who ever heard of a woman pastor? I hadn't. Besides that, I had been divorced before I was saved. I had sought God's will in that decision, even though I was not yet saved. Divorce would certainly disqualify me, wouldn't it? I continually stuffed the promptings of the Holy Spirit I was feeling. I tried to talk my husband Dell into being a pastor and he kept saying he wasn't called. We attended the Institute of Ministry in Bradenton, Florida and completed that. I wanted us to stay and attend the Pastor's School, but Dell wasn't at all interested, so we didn't.

It wasn't until two years after Dell passed away and I was married to Jerry that the Lord spoke to me and said, "When will you stop making excuses and just do what I told you to do?"

When I heard Him say that, I instantly said, "Right now, God!" Within a few months, we started a church.

I can really relate to Moses. Let's look at his experience. One would think that because his call was so dramatic, he would instantly respond with, "Yes, Sir!" That was not the case. Let's take a closer look at Exodus 3. Moses was at work on an ordinary day. He was tending the flock of his father-in-law on the backside of the desert. God appeared to him as an Angel of the Lord in a flame of fire from the middle of a bush! As he looked, he saw that the fire wasn't consuming the bush, although the flame of fire was coming from the middle of the bush.

Moses turned off the beaten path to get a better look at the bush to see why it wasn't being consumed. That impressed God enough that He called to him from the middle of the bush, *"Moses! Moses!"*

Moses responded with, *"Here I am."* That's the best response to God that I can think of when you sense He is calling your name.

God proceeded to tell Moses who He is, that where Moses was standing was holy, and not to come any closer. He continued by telling him that He had seen the oppression of His people in Egypt and had heard their cries and knew their sorrows, and had come down to deliver them out of their bondage. Isn't it encouraging to know that? God sees!

God hears! God knows! He comes down to deliver us and take us into our promise! God invited Moses to come with Him and be sent to Pharaoh to bring His people out of bondage. Ministry is normally born out of need.

Moses responded just like most of us. *"Who am I?"* He judged himself unworthy, inadequate, incompetent, and insignificant. Just like Moses, many of us have been carrying a spirit of "feeling less than"; less than able, less than qualified, less important than, less gifted than. Our own self-judgments have kept us from moving toward our destiny. We need to repent of believing those lies of the devil and repent of any agreement we have made with those lies, as well as repent of all the energy we have given them. We then renounce the lies, and receive the cleansing blood and the healing we need from Jesus so we close the door of vulnerability in that area. We can then allow the Spirit of God to flood us with His plans, His power and His ability!

Jesus came to heal the brokenhearted. Many times our hearts have been broken in pieces by the hurts and traumas we have experienced. A part of our soul has actually been damaged or broken off.

The healing comes when you ask Holy Spirit to show you the root of your pain or brokenness; to show you, in your mind, a picture of yourself when you were first experiencing the feeling of insignificance, or incompetence, or unworthiness.

Holy Spirit is faithful to do it. As you picture that child or baby or young adult that looks like you, go to that one (in your mind) and put your arm around him or her. Ask Jesus to come to that one. Experience how Jesus feels about him or her. Renounce any agreement with the devil, concerning who you are. Renounce giving him any energy and command him to give back to Jesus any energy you have given him. Take authority over the spirits that entered in at that time. Ask Jesus to restore that one emotionally, mentally and in every part of his or her being; then invite him or her to be restored back into your heart, and let him or her just melt back in.

Healing that part of your soul will allow you to move on toward your destiny. As I was was doing the final editing on this chapter, I asked the Lord if there was a part of me that needed to be rescued. Instantly, I saw myself as a child of four years old, hiding behind my mom's skirt. As I went to that one (in my mind's eye) and looked into her heart, I saw fear, shame, incompetence, insignificance, and unworthiness. I saw that I was actually ashamed of who I was. I asked Jesus to come to that little girl. Instantly He came, picked her up and swung her around! Then he put her on His shoulders. Suddenly I felt ten feet tall! Then I renounced my agreement with the enemy about who I was. I renounced giving him any energy and commanded him to give to Jesus every bit of energy I had given him. I took authority over every negative spirit that entered at that time and commanded it to go where the Lord Jesus Christ sends it! I then asked Jesus to restore my dignity, self-respect, self-worth, and confidence, and restore that part of my soul back into my heart. What a release I experienced!

Notice God's response to Moses' question, *"Who am I?"* God answers, *"I will certainly be with you."* It's not about who you are. It's about having God with you. The less we look at us and the more we look at God, Who lives in us, and His abilities, the more successful we will be. I heard many years ago, "You can't be self-conscious and God-conscious at the same time." If you're consumed with looking at you, you won't see how big God is.

Moses' next question is, *"What do I tell the people your name is?"*

God answered, *"I AM WHO I AM."* In other words, "I AM YAHWEH, the God Who is actively present with you."

Wow! That should cause us to take a leap of faith! Soon after you do, the next attack will normally come. This one usually comes from your own brothers and sisters, either in the natural or in the Lord. It's called, "Who are you?"

Even Jesus encountered this mindset. Jesus was teaching in the temple and preaching the gospel.

> *The chief priests and the scribes, together with the elders, confronted Him and spoke to Him saying, "Tell us, by what authority are You doing these things? Or who is he who gave You this authority?"* (Luke 20:1 & 2)

All the chief priests and elders of the people plotted against Jesus to put Him to death. Jesus knew that they had handed him over because of envy. Jesus had been doing awesome things that had not been happening in their own ministries. He had been healing the sick, raising the dead, casting out demons, multiplying a few pieces of food to feed many thousands of people, and stilling the wind. He made them look like powerless wimps. They felt threatened that they would lose their ministries if they didn't stop Jesus. Even though they believed all the prophecies of the Old Testament about the Savior coming, they didn't recognize Him when He was right there in front of them.

This often happens in the church today. We keep praying Holy Spirit will come and when He shows up, because He doesn't manifest in the way we're comfortable with, we don't recognize Him. Therefore we don't welcome Him and give Him room to move, so He isn't comfortable in our presence. He leaves and goes where he is welcomed.

Remember when Joseph shared his dream with his brothers? They responded with, "Shall you reign over us?" His brothers envied him and sought, from that moment on, to get rid of him.

When Nehemiah saw the condition of Jerusalem, he prayed and fasted until he got the word from the Lord. He scouted it out first, then gathered the Jews, priests, nobles, officials and others and said,

> "Come and let us build the wall of Jerusalem that we may no longer be a reproach." (Nehemiah 2:17b)

He told them of God's hand being upon him, and they responded, "Let us rise up and build." Then they immediately got to work. God gave Nehemiah favor with the king and with those who would supply all the materials.

Immediately Sanballat and Tobiah were there mocking them, saying, "What are you doing? Are you rebelling against the king?" I love Nehemiah's response, which should also be ours.

> "The God of heaven Himself will prosper us; therefore we His servants will arise and build." (Nehemiah 2:20a)

Sanballat and Tobiah didn't stop. They continued mocking them, trying to get them to question themselves. They gathered others and conspired together to try to stop the work. They tried to sneak into their midst to destroy them. They even offered to help so they could get into the midst of them. Nehemiah gathered warriors and said to all the people.

> *"Do not be afraid of them. Remember the Lord, great and awesome, and fight for your brothers, your sons, your daughters, your wives and your houses."* (Nehemiah 4:14)

This is key. Remember how great and awesome the Lord is. Continue to fight for your fellow people and for future generations. Remember, others are dependent on you fulfilling your destiny!

So half worked at construction and half did the warring. Even the builders had their swords at their side. We need spiritual warriors to pray for us and fight for us. There are no lone rangers in God's army. The warriors are just as important as the builders, because we can't build when darts are hitting us from every direction. Surround yourself with mighty warriors who will fight for you. You continue to build and do warfare also.

Know that your enemy the devil wants to destroy, not only your dreams and destiny, but he wants to destroy the house. If you knew a thief, a killer, and a destroyer were coming to your house, would you not get ready with all of the weapons you could find? Wouldn't you be sure the doors and windows were securely locked? Surely we should be even more prepared to protect our house that God inhabits and empowers. It's our responsibility to determine what comes in and what stays out.

> *For though we walk in the flesh, we do not war according to the flesh. For the weapons of our warfare are not carnal but mighty in God for pulling down of strongholds.* (II Corinthians 10:3,4)

Strongholds are merely anything that seems to have a strong hold, opposing God's will and purpose. Fleshly weapons like manipulation or intimidation won't work. They just feed energy into the enemy camp. We need God-empowered weapons to demolish strongholds.

God has equipped us with His armor. We need to put it all on and use it so we'll be able to stand against the devil's strategies to deceive, entrap, and ensnare. We're not to fight against individual people, but we are to engage actively against principalities and powers and rulers of darkness, which are working behind the scenes, where we can't see in the natural.

What is this armor? It's found in Ephesians 6:10-18

1. **Take your stand firmly in the truth.** The devil will send you lies to distract you or stop you. Ask yourself frequently, "What's the truth?" "Does what you're hearing line up with God's Word and God's character?" If not, stand against the lie and keep speaking the truth! The truth is your belt. It holds all the rest of your armor in place.
2. **Put on the breastplate of righteousness.** Righteousness is conformity to the revealed will of God. Jesus has placed on me His righteousness. He is my righteousness. He became sin for me that I would become the righteousness of God in Christ Jesus. II Corinthians 5:21 I can't earn it. I don't have to work at it. I just need to believe it and receive it. The breastplate covers your heart to protect it. Standing in His righteousness will repel attacks of guilt, condemnation, and unworthiness.
3. **Walk out the good news of peace wherever you go.** Be prepared. Be saturated with His Word, His presence, and His power wherever the Holy Spirit directs you to go. Release His peace and His glory as you go.
4. **Take the helmet of salvation.** This covers your mind, which is the real battleground, with the truth of salvation, which is much more than freedom from judgment of Hell and a ticket to Heaven. The very word salvation includes: Forgiveness, justification, preservation, liberty, healing, restoration, protection, and deliverance. Whenever the

enemy attacks your mind, you remind him of all that you have received in your salvation.

5. **Take the sword of the Spirit.** This is your offensive weapon, the Word of God. It's so powerful that the whole next chapter will be devoted to this one.
6. **Pray always with all prayer and supplication in the Spirit.** Don't pray soulish prayers, praying off the top of your head what you want and how you want it to happen. Worship God. Pray in the Spirit. Then pray what you hear the Father say, whatever He puts on your heart. Supplication is fully transferring the burden into God's hands. Trust Him to answer. He is fully willing and able to take care of it.

Let's look back to Moses in Exodus 3:16-22. God gave him specific instructions. "Go and gather the elders of Israel. Let them know God has surely visited them and has seen what is happening to them. Tell them I will bring them out of their affliction. I will take you in to a land flowing with milk and honey. It won't happen right away. You just follow My instructions. Every bit of resistance is an opportunity for My wonders and miracles which I'll do in the midst of you. After that, you'll be free, and you won't go empty-handed. I will give you great favor and you shall plunder your enemy."

Moses still questioned, "What if they won't believe me or listen to me?" Me, me, me. It's all about me. God demonstrated His authority. He demonstrated His power. Moses still made excuses.

"I'm slow of speech. I'm slow of tongue." (Exodus 4:10)

He still focused on himself and his inadequacies. The Lord brought the focus back to Himself.

"Who made your mouth? Who makes the mute, the deaf, the seeing or the blind? Have not I the Lord?" (Exodus 4:12)

Moses still told him to send somebody else. God got angry! God doesn't get angry at us, but for us! He wants much more for us than we want for ourselves! As with Moses, a whole nation may be depending upon us.

Many times we give up just before the victory. Nine times Moses saw no positive response when he followed the instructions of the Lord and went before Pharaoh. The tenth time, there was great victory for the whole nation! We need great tenacity to see great victory! Many times you may have to do the ridiculous to see the miraculous!

Embrace your destiny! You don't know how many will be impacted!

CHAPTER FOUR

THE POWER WEAPON

There are often strange sounds in your house. These sounds can destroy, even right down to the foundation. If you start giving ear to the sounds, and worse yet, give voice to the sounds, it will empower the devil to destroy the house.

God has given us an amazingly powerful weapon! It's so simple to use that we often miss it. Your power weapon is merely speaking what God speaks. Just as Jesus used the word of God against the devil in Luke 4 and he was defeated, it will work the same for us. Arguing with the devil is useless. Speak the Word of God against him.

> *For the Word that God speaks is alive and full of power {making it active, operative, energizing, and effective}; it is sharper than any two-edged sword; penetrating to the dividing line of the breath of life {soul} and {the immortal} spirit, and of joints and marrow {of the deepest parts of our nature, exposing and sifting and analyzing and judging the very thoughts and purposes of the heart.* (Hebrews 4:12 Amplified Bible)

I love how the Amplified Bible reads in this verse. For the Word that God speaks. I believe we have been limiting ourselves and limiting God. As He speaks a rhema word to us, it has great power! That power is increased and released as we continue to speak what we have been hearing Him speak. It's alive and full of power!

I've always felt there was more to this scripture than I understood and I had a desire to more fully understand it. A couple of years ago, when I was at a Mountaintop Believers Conference at Big Bear with A.L. and Joyce Gill, during the awesome worship, I suddenly had a vision of the word of God. The letters were huge, and as I would speak the rhema word of God back to Him, the words became alive and breathing and even dancing and they would go forth to that to whom I sent it and it would penetrate their very being and become alive in them! It was an awesome revelation!

As I was driving down the mountain, everything I prayed for were things I'd been praying for a long time. As I sent forth the word of God with increased faith and zeal, all those things came to pass within a few days. No other words have power like that!

Many years ago, on September 26, 1990, I had a very real dream. I was speaking in a large auditorium to a huge crowd of people. In the dream I was aware that I was speaking from John 5 and Acts 5. Then the one who was leading the meeting came to me and said, "Kay, we're running out of time. What is the main point you want the people to remember?" Instantly the words came out of my mouth, "Do only what God has told you to do!" In the dream the words burned in me as I spoke them. Then I woke up, with those words burning in my heart. I hurried to my Bible to check the two chapters. The following verses confirmed God's message.

> Jesus said, *"I can of Myself do nothing. As I hear, I judge; and My judgment is righteous, because I do not seek My own will but the will of the Father who sent Me.* (John 5:30)

> Jesus answered and said to them, "Most assuredly I say to you, the Son can do nothing of Himself, but what He sees the Father do; for whatever He does, the Son also does in like manner." (John 5:19)

If Jesus only did what He saw and heard the Father do, that's exactly what we should do if we want the kind of results that Jesus got.

> But Peter and the other apostles answered and said: "We ought to obey God rather than men." (Acts 5:29)

I then felt inspired to write the following poem:

Listen, My child, to all that is true
Hear what I say and do what I do.
Miracles daily will happen to you
As you hear what I say and do what I do.

The pressure's been on to destroy you, My child.
In Satan's sick mind, it's his will.
But I've called you out of his realm of power,
So come away with Me and be still.

At the end of yourself is the beginning of Me.
That's where I AM and will stay.
Turn loose of it all and rise up with Me
And you'll do what I do when you hear what I say.

In Mark 12:29 Jesus was asked, *"Which is the first commandment of all?"*

He quoted Deuteronomy 6:4:

"Hear, O Israel, the Lord our God, The Lord is One."

Hear is the Hebrew word shm'a, which means hear intelligently with implication to attention; attentively call together carefully, consider, consent, discern, listen, obey, perceive, proclaim, show forth. I have been told by Hebrew scholars that this is the highest form of prayer in Judaism and everyday they stand and recite this prayer.

Israel means led by God.

This shows us that those who are led by God are expected to hear, not only what He has already said, but also what He is presently saying. This enables you to love the Lord your God with all your heart and with all your soul and all your strength, and love your neighbor as yourself. In any valuable relationship, it is imperative to hear that loved one's thoughts and feelings and concerns. Lack of those entities would produce a shallow relationship.

God is looking for people who will hear what He is saying. Without that, there are no fresh revelations, no vision, no relationship and no acts of God being performed; only complacency and religion.

In February 1993 I had a dream of a major earthquake. In the dream I kept hearing on the radio and on the TV and through many voices, "There's a major earthquake coming! There's a major earthquake coming!". It shook me and when I awoke, I asked the Lord if that was Him. He answered, "Yes, I'm coming in calamity to separate the wheat from the chaff." I asked, "God, what do you want me to do?" He answered, "Teach people to hear My voice. Those who have learned to hear My voice will be safe."

Later that day, I went downtown to a beauty supply store. I encountered a friend named Abe. His opening line was, "You're not going to believe what I dreamed last night!" I almost fell over because instantly I knew what he was going to say! He said, "I dreamed there was a major earthquake!" I asked, "Did it actually happen in your dream?" He said, "Yes, and there was devastation everywhere." I found out later that another of my friends, a pastor's wife named Donna, had the same dream on the same night.

I don't know when or where that earthquake will take place, but the there is one thing I am positive about. It is imperative to learn to hear the voice of the Lord, and it has been a priority with me, since that time, to teach people to hear His voice for their own safety.

From Genesis through Revelations God spoke and we are told to hear or to listen. Genesis 1:26,27, Genesis 6:9-12, Genesis 12:1,3, Exodus 3:1-14, Joshua 1:1-9, John 5:19,30, Proverbs 1:33, 2:1-6, 7:24, 8:6, Isaiah 55:3,4, 33:3, 34:1, 42:23, 48:12, Mich 1:2, Hebrews 12:25,26

Throughout Revelation, Jesus says,

"To Him that has ears to hear, let him hear!"

Then He gave promises to him that overcomes. Overcome is a military term suggesting combat against the enemy. Do we all have ears to hear? How well do we hear? How well do we listen? We have a spiritual ear and a natural ear.

How does God communicate with you? By His Word, by a prompting or impression or picture, by a still, small voice, by dreams and visions or by a prophetic word. He can even use a movie or a message.

In Mark 4:3-11 Jesus begins by commanding, "Listen!" Then He describes four kinds of people. Verse 15 says the first hears, but allows Satan to come immediately and take away the word he heard. I liken this to having earwax in the natural ear, which doesn't allow words to penetrate. Through rationalizing or doubting, or fear or anger, or pride, we've allowed Satan to block the word of the Lord from penetrating into us and becoming alive. We blow it off. We need to clean out our spiritual ears regularly so our hearing isn't blocked. Satan tries very diligently to steal the word God has spoken to each of us, and often we have allowed him to do it.

The second group of people, described in verse 16 and 17, gets all excited about what God says, but they are not rooted in the truth and in the love of Christ. They hang onto it for a little while, but when the going gets rough, they immediately stumble and let go of that word. A stony heart is a hardened heart due to hurts and disappointments, judgments, wrong perceptions of Who God is, who you are, or who others are.

Persecution and tribulation are sent by the enemy to cause you to let go of what God has said. I liken this to an ear injury in the natural, which prohibits you from hearing correctly. Satan sends an injury or offense to cause you to get angry and offended. It will block the flow of that wonderful word and hinder it from continuing to work in you.

The third group, described in verses 18 and 19, is the people who hear the word, and allow the cares of this world, the deceitfulness of riches, and the desires for other things, which choke out the word, and it then becomes unfruitful. I liken this to an ear infection in the natural, caused by foreign matter in the wrong place.

It's so easy to get distracted. The cares of the world are many times good things, but wrongly prioritized. It may be work, housework, your mate, children, friends, hobbies, or any other interests, which are good, but if they take first place over what God is telling you to do, then the word of the Lord gets stifled or snuffed out.

The deceitfulness of riches is so prevalent in the United States. We want more stuff that the devil makes us think we must have in order to be really happy. We max out our credit cards with our wants and then have to work hard to pay even the monthly payments to keep our heads above water. Our work then consumes all of our time and energy, and we miss what God is saying to us.

The desires for other things can be popularity, fame, fortune, or anything that drains you of passion and desire for God. Anything or anyone you love more than God, or give priority to above God, is an idol. If you hold onto an idol, you will hear everything through that idol, and the truth will be distorted or perverted. What do you get passionate about?

Jesus continued on to say in Mark 12,

"And you shall love the Lord your God with all your heart, with all your soul, with all your mind, and with all your strength. This is the first commandment."

It's much easier to get passionate about someone you can hear and have a relationship with. That's why God gave us a spiritual ear. Jesus said,

"My sheep hear My voice and I know them and they follow Me." (John 10:27)

The word hear denotes repeated or habitual activity; hear and keep on hearing. How do you sharpen hearing? Like any other skill, you must practice.

How do you distinguish the voice of the Lord from the voice of the devil or your own voice? What does His voice sound like?

It brings life, not death. It brings peace, not anxiety. It will be truth in love, not verbally beating you up. It will be enlightening, because God is light. It will not contradict the Word of God. It's the sound of faith, stretching you beyond your comfort level.

It's the sound of love, of unconditional love. He even reprimands with love.

It's the sound of kindness and goodness. It's the sound of faithfulness, because God is always faithful.

It's the sound of gentleness, because God is never pushy.

It's the sound of grace and mercy, not of harsh judgment, because God is a merciful God.

It's the sound of unity, of synergy, because God is calling His real followers to flow together as one, as each one operates in his own unique gifting and ability. Will it benefit only you or others in the body as well? Does it flow with what other trusted saints are hearing and saying?

A couple of years ago, Pastor Dennis Walker was ministering in our church on "Catching the Initiatives of Heaven"; in other words, hearing and seeing what God is doing and then, doing it and seeing miracles. He was sharing testimonies of how it works. All while I was listening to him, I kept seeing, in my spirit, a throbbing toe. I kept thinking, "I'm not going to say anything. Pastor Dennis is ministering." Suddenly he stopped and asked, "Is anyone else seeing anything?"

I quickly replied, "That would be me."

"Come up here!" he commanded. I jumped up and stood beside him. He asked, "What are you seeing?"

"I keep seeing a throbbing toe."

"Who has a throbbing toe?" Dennis asked.

A very large man named Mike, who was sitting in the back row, raised his hand. Dennis asked me, "What do you see God doing?"

With my thumb and forefinger I showed him and said, "I see Him flick it like that." At that, Dennis said, "Go, do it."

I was hesitant and responded, "Moi?" After all, the last thing anyone with a throbbing toe would want would be someone flicking it, right?

Dennis reasoned, "You're the one God showed. You're the one to do it."

I went to the back of the church to Mike. I asked him which toe, bent down and flicked his toe, and instantly his toe stopped hurting and it was healed!

Another story comes to mind of when I was in Peru a few years ago in a service. Wes, who was on our ministry team, got a word that the Lord was going to heal a baby that night. Dennis started preaching and a baby began screaming and continued while Dennis was trying to preach. Suddenly Dennis stopped and directed some of us to go to the back with the baby. The first thing we did was to ask God what His initiative was for the baby's healing. I felt impressed that it was a stomach disorder that was actually a birth defect. God impressed upon me that if I would pick the baby up and turn her upside down, He would heal that stomach. The lady didn't speak English and I spoke very little Spanish. Lynnie asked the lady in Spanish if I could hold her baby. She said I could. I then took the baby and, very gently and slowly, put her up over my shoulder and tipped her upside down. She instantly stopped crying!

The next day we ran into the lady at the market. She told Lynnie that before that night the baby never slept. She would scream every night. After our ministry to her, the baby never cried at all and she had slept all night!

We often have to do the ridiculous in order to see the miraculous. Why does God work that way? I believe it's because He chooses to and because we have to get our pride out of the way and be dependent upon God in order to do it.

How did Jesus heal blind eyes? With the two things you would never want in your eyes, spit and dirt.

All through the Old Testament, we can see the strategy for victory was simply to do what God said to do. Most times, God's instructions seemed trivial or silly to the natural mind.

Remember the battle of Jericho when God gave Joshua specific instructions? He told them to march around the city one time for six days, and, on the seventh day, to march seven times around the city. Then the priests were to blow the trumpets, all the people were to shout and the wall of the city would fall down flat. Joshua commanded the people to not make any noise with their mouths until he told them to shout. He wanted no murmuring as often had done in the past. He didn't want them speaking their fear, doubt, and unbelief. When they obeyed, the wall fell down flat and they went up and took the city. Isn't that an amazing way to conquer a city?

In Judges 6 and 7, when the children of Israel cried out to the Lord because of the attacks of their enemies, God sent an angel to call Gideon to lead His mighty army against the Midianites and Amalekites. He said, "The Lord is with you, you mighty man of valor!" Gideon's response sounded the opposite of a mighty man! He found many excuses why he couldn't lead an army. Gideon started with 32,000 in his army. God said, "No, that's too many," and eliminated all but 300, who were divided into three companies of one hundred. He didn't want that army to claim the glory for winning on its own. He wanted to get all the glory for the victory!

The designated weapons were a trumpet in one hand and an empty pitcher containing a torch in the other. That sounds ridiculous, doesn't it? How would you like to face a wicked army with only a trumpet and a torch?

At the direction of the Lord, as every man stood in his place, they all blew the trumpets and broke the pitchers and shouted, "The sword of the Lord and of Gideon!" The whole enemy army cried out and fled and turned on each other! How powerful are broken vessels of light who will listen, respond and simply do as God directs!

What you are listening to determines who you are listening to. For instance, you may have listened to a voice in your head saying, "If they had to go through a little suffering, they'd see things the way I see them." Were you listening to the Father of love or the father of bitterness?

Maybe you've listened to this voice, "How are you ever going to pay these bills? We'll never get out of debt!" Were you listening to the Father of provision or the father of lack and doubt?

How about this one? "Your life is just falling apart! What are you going to do now?" Is that voice the Father of peace or the father of anxiety and worry?

Here's a familiar one. "No one understands me. No one cares about what I'm feeling. No one really loves me" Is that the voice of the Father of truth Who is Truth or is it the father of lies?

Let's look at John 8. According to verse 31, Jesus is speaking to those Jews who believed in Him. They are making false accusations against Jesus. In verse 44 Jesus said,

> *"You are of your father the devil, and the desires of your father you want to do. He was a murderer from the beginning, and does not stand in the truth, because there is no truth in him. When he speaks a lie, he speaks from his own resources, for he is a liar and the father of it."*

Some of the voices that we listen to in our heads come right from the father of lies. We are responsible for what we are listening to and entertaining.

If, in the church, we entertained a drunk and disorderly guy and allowed him to speak, from the microphone, against God or against the people or against himself, would you not say that we were dishonoring God?

So, therefore, if we allow the devil to speak to us negatively about God, or negatively about others in the church, or negatively about ourselves, couldn't we say that we are dishonoring God in this temple? You are the temple of the Holy Spirit. You are the house of God.

> *"Or do you not know that your body is the temple of the Holy Spirit who is in you, whom you have from God, and not your own?"* (1 Corinthians 6:19)

> *"So then faith comes by hearing, and hearing by the word of God."* (Romans 10:17)

Faith comes by hearing God. Fear, doubt, and unbelief come by hearing the devil. It's part of my inheritance to hear God! It's part of your inheritance to hear God. God calls us to listen! In Isaiah 55:2b & 3 God says:

> *"Listen carefully to Me, and eat what is good, and let your soul delight itself in abundance. Incline your ear, and come to Me. Hear, and your soul shall live; And I will make an everlasting covenant with you- the sure mercies of David."*

God promises us if we listen carefully to Him, we'll chew on what is beneficial, and our minds, wills, and emotions will delight in abundance! What God says is life-giving to me and to you. Incline is an interesting word. How do you incline your ear? Lay it on His chest. Lean into Him. Hear His heartbeat for you and for His people!

Before you act, ask God to show you what He is doing. Ask God what He is saying. Do or say accordingly, even it it seems ridiculous. As you move with God, you'll see awesome things happen! You'll be releasing His life into people and situations everywhere you go!

CHAPTER FIVE

PREPARATION FOR GREATNESS

Much preparation is needed in order to build a great house. Much is to be considered before beginning to build, such as each of the materials needed, the quantity needed, the time and energy it will take, and, more importantly, the cost of completion. There is a great distinction between the preparation necessary for building a mud hut and the preparation necessary for a presidential palace. So it is for this house God is building. How much we submit to the preparation will determine the greatness of the house. This leads me to one of my favorite stories, which is about David and Goliath.

In I Samuel 16 we read of how the Lord spoke to Samuel and told him to take the anointing oil and go to Jesse's house. He said, "For I have provided Myself a king among his sons."

Samuel assumed it would surely be the eldest son Eliab, but the Lord said to Samuel,

> *"Do not look at his appearance or at his physical stature, because I have refused him. For the Lord does not see as man sees; for man looks at the outward appearance, but the Lord looks at the heart."* (I Samuel 16:7)

That's important for us to remember. God may choose a boy or girl with blue and purple hair who is covered with tattoos and has a pound of hardware attached to his or her face. He could raise him or her up to be a mighty leader! Who are we to judge by appearance? It's all about the heart. Does he or she have a listening heart in tune with the heartbeat of God for His people? God was, and still is, looking for Himself a man or woman after His own heart.

Samuel went down the line of Jesse's sons and God rejected them all. Then he asked, "Are all the young men here?"

Jesse said, "There's the youngest who is keeping the sheep." In other words, "There's the insignificant one."

Samuel said, "Send for him and bring him. We're not moving until he comes here!" When he was brought in, the Lord said,

> *"Arise, anoint him; for this is the one!"* (1 Samuel 16:12)

Imagine that! The least likely one in the natural is the one God chose to anoint! Samuel anointed him in the midst of his brothers. Do you think they may have been a little bit jealous of David? I'm sure of it! The Spirit of the Lord came upon David from that day forward.

Because King Saul had disobeyed God and didn't follow through with what God said, the Spirit of the Lord departed from Saul and a distressing spirit from the Lord came upon him. His servants suggested he send for David to play his harp for him and whenever David played, the distressing spirit left Saul and he would become refreshed. There is tremendous power in anointed worship! The anointing was on David and upon his worship.

Each one is anointed for a calling and a destiny. We are called to be the mighty army of the Lord. In Revelations chapter two, all the promises are "To him who overcomes", so obviously He has adequately equipped us. In all successful warfare, it is vitally urgent that we familiarize ourselves with the strategy of the enemy to defeat us, as well as the strategy of the Lord for victory. Both are found in the study of David and Goliath. Each of us will meet some giants, who look much larger than we are and roar much louder. Will we be overtaken by these seemingly insurmountable trials and challenges, or will we, like David coming up against Goliath, know our God, and, in His power, defeat the giants of our life triumphantly?

In 1 Samuel 17, we find that the Israelites (led by God) were in battle against the Philistines (flesh). This is an on-going battle for us today.

The flesh wars against the Spirit and the Spirit wars against the flesh. (Galatians 5:17)

Each army stood on a mountain with a valley in between. Out of the camp of the Philistines came a giant Rambo named Goliath. He was nearly ten feet tall and covered from head to toe with heavy bronze armor. His bronze coat alone weighed 126 pounds. He had a bronze javelin and just his spearhead weighed between fifteen and sixteen pounds.

Seeing Goliath must have been as terrifying as looking out the windshield of your little Smart Car into the face of a huge Mack truck, speeding recklessly toward you.

He was intimidating enough to look at, but then he opened his big mouth and cried out to the armies of Israel,

"Why have you come out to line up for battle? Am I not a Philistine, and you the servants of Saul? Choose a man for yourselves, and let him come down to me. If he is able to fight with me and kill me, then we will be your servants. But if I prevail against him and kill him, then you shall be our servants and serve us. I defy the armies of Israel this day; give me a man, that we may fight together." (I Samuel 17:9-10)

When King Saul and all Israel heard these words, they were dismayed and greatly afraid. (1 Samuel 17:11)

The definition of dismayed in this passage is: amazing terror that confounds the faculties of the mind; the reverse of the mind under the influence of joy, hope and confidence; disabled with alarm. This would be one depressed mind! Though they were God's mighty army, they had more faith in their enemy than faith in God. Note that it was threatening words that caused depression and fear. They were a lot like us. Do your giants ever sound so boisterous and look so humongous that you feel disabled? What giants in your life are intimidating you? What causes you to be depressed and fearful? With each of us, the giant may be different.

It could be unemployment or a negative physical prognosis. It could be a fear of failure or fear of disapproval or fear of rejection or abandonment or a fear of what God will ask of you or fear of what man can do to you. Fears can emotionally or mentally paralyze you. What giant comes at you and taunts you, making you feel helpless and hopeless?

One strategy of the enemy is to cause you to feel depressed, disabled, paralyzed, like a tiny ball of fuzz, lying helplessly in the path of a zooming powerful vacuum cleaner!

I remember thirty years ago when I felt really intimidated by a particular young woman. On my way to her house one day a song rose up within me and, as I sang it, I was no longer intimidated.

The song goes like this:

I will not be intimidated! No! No! No!
I will not be intimidated! No! No! No!
Satan, you can keep your stuff!
I will not receive your guff!
I will not be intimidated! No! No! No!

I recognized my problem was not the lady, but I realized I had been harassed by an intimidating spirit. I never again battled that intimidating spirit with that lady, and anytime I would feel intimidated by anyone else and I would sing the little song, the intimidating spirit would leave.

Goliath would come out morning and evening for forty days, repeating the same threats. Isn't that just how Satan works? He keeps roaring in your ears, repeating the same negative words over and over to try to make you believe a lie and to make you afraid because he wants to steal your faith and cause you to miss your assignments and your destiny.

David was the youngest of Jesse's eight sons. The three oldest sons followed Saul to battle. One day Jesse sent David with food for his brothers. As he approached the camp, the army was going out to the fight and shouting the battle cry. All the mighty warriors, including the king and all the men of Israel, were there.

As he talked with his brothers, Goliath, this champion of the Philistine, came out and he spoke the same terrifying words, so David heard them. All the men of Israel fled from him and were dreadfully afraid. These were the mighty warriors? All of them fled? All were terrified? At the sound of Goliath's scary threats, the confidence of these skilled warriors slipped away like air from a balloon pricked by a sharp knife.

When we look at our problem with the natural eye and see it as overpowering, how do we react? Do we run and hide? Do we cry out to God, "Make it go away! This is too big for me!"? Or do we react like David did?

The Israeli men were talking about the rewards for one who would kill Goliath. The king promised to enrich him with great riches, give him his daughter, and give his father's house exemption from taxes. What man wouldn't want to be enriched with great riches, be part of the royal family and eliminate paying taxes? I'm sure all the men wanted that!

> *David asked the men, "What will be done for the man who kills this Philistine and takes away the disgrace from Israel? For who is this uncircumcised Philistine, that he should defy the armies of the living God?"* (I Samuel 17:26)

In other words, "Who does he think he is, trying to bully God's people?"

David recognized that Goliath was the enemy of the armies of the living God. It's important that we recognize quickly who our real enemy is. It's not people. It's the devil working through whoever is available. What's his purpose? To steal, kill, and destroy from the armies of God. Who's the commander of our army? The living God! Who can defeat Him? No one! We are in a war. It's not time to surrender to the enemy! It's time to stand up in the power of the Lord Jesus Christ and take authority over the enemy! David is saying, "How dare this guy think he can defy the armies of the living God!" Defy means to challenge to combat; to challenge to do something considered impossible; to confront with assured power of resistance.

David was human like us, but he set his attention and his affections on God and His ability to deliver! David had spent time getting to know His God. He was totally confident that He was not only able, but perfectly willing to deliver His people. He knew God is a good God! Because of that, David knew who he was, part of the army of the living God, even though he was a young boy, who no one else considered to be part of the army. David recognized his real enemy and his place under David's feet.

We are to know our God...know who we are...and recognize our enemy and his place under our feet!

> *Withstand him; be firm in faith {against his onset – rooted, established, strong, immovable, and determined}, knowing that the same (identical) sufferings are appointed to your brotherhood (the whole body of Christians) throughout the world.* (I Peter 5:9 Amplified Bible)

> *Jesus said, "Behold, I have given you authority and power to trample upon serpents and scorpions and {physical and mental strength and ability} over all the power that the enemy {possesses} and nothing shall in any way harm you.* (Luke 10:19 Amplified Bible)

> *For whatever is born of God is victorious over the world and this is the victory that conquers the world, even our faith.* (I John 5:4)

We have been given His Word to stand on, and we have been given the authority and the power to trample out all the power of the enemy! We must be firm in faith to believe it and act upon it!

Who's the commander of our army? The living God! Who can defeat Him? No one! We are in a war. It's not time to surrender to the enemy! It's certainly not time to compromise in any way. It's time to stand up in the power of the Lord Jesus Christ and take authority over the enemy!

When David stepped up to the plate, he stepped out in faith, and look what manifested itself: Envy from those closest to him.

The people told David of the three rewards. Eliab, David's oldest brother heard him asking and became very angry!

> *He said, "Why have you come down here? And with whom have you left those few sheep in the wilderness? I know your pride and the insolence of your heart, for you have come down to see the battle."* (I Samuel 17:28)

He was jealous of David's bravery and boldness, so he implied David's job was menial, and that he was prideful, overbearing, insulting, and had an evil heart. When you're willing to go where others won't, there will be those who are envious and try to stop you from getting there.

There are some familiar attacks here. Eliab attacked his motive. He insinuated David was irresponsible. He made false accusations about pride and showing off. Then he again attacked David's motive. When you take a leap of faith, the devil will use these tactics to try to stop you. He invents lies that are the direct opposite of the truth. God had said David was a man after His own heart, so Satan attacked David with the lie that his heart was evil. Did David react negatively to jealousy and false accusations? No, he didn't! He chose not to be offended. The definition of offense is "the part of the trap that holds the bait." We can't afford to go there. We must be dead to self, alive unto God!

> *And David said, "What have I done now? Is there not a cause?"* (I Samuel 17:29)

That is a question we should ask ourselves. **Is there not a cause?** It wasn't about him. It was about his nation. It was about God's people and God's purpose. It's not about me. It's not about you. It's about God's kingdom coming to this region and to this nation as it is in heaven! It's about leaving the future generations a better place to live. It's about keeping people from spending eternity in hell. Is there not a cause? " 'Cause God commands" is reason enough for me.

> *"Be bold! Be strong! For the Lord your God is with you!"* (Joshua 1:9)

David asked other people about the king's rewards. They all answered him the same way, with accusations and attacks. Did that deter David? Did he get discouraged and rejected and quit? No, he did not! The people reported him to King Saul and the king sent for him. Did he go in fear and trembling? No! It was David who began the conversation first. He took an offensive position rather than a defensive one. He was a young man, not even qualified for the king's army, yet he was bold and brave and looked right into the king's face and declared,

> *"Let no man's heart fail because of Goliath; your servant will go and fight with this Philistine."* (I Samuel 17:32)

In other words, he was saying, "Don't anyone have a heart attack! I serve the living God and His people and I will go and fight Goliath! Faith with humility is powerful!

Saul responded in the flesh.

> *"You aren't able to go against this Philistine to fight with him; for you are a youth, and he a man of war from his youth."* (I Samuel 17:33)

"After all," he was saying, "Goliath is humongous and he's got massive powerful armor and he's very experienced. You're just an inexperienced kid! We've never even done this before!"

Did David react to the insults or the rejection? No! Did he allow any thoughts of past discouragements or defeats? No! Fear, doubt, and unbelief came against him! He chose to ignore them and concentrate on his past victories and he began speaking of them. He told of how when he was keeping his father's sheep and a lion or bear came and took a lamb out of the flock he went after it and attacked it and delivered the lamb from its mouth. When it attacked him, he caught it by its beard and struck and killed it. He spoke his faith and said,

> "Your servant has killed both lion and bear; and this uncircumcised Philistine will be like one of them, seeing he has defied the armies of the living God. The Lord who delivered me from the paw of the lion and from the paw of the bear, He will deliver me from the hand of this Philistine." (I Samuel 17:34-37)

When I'm about to pray for someone in dire need of a big miracle, I choose to tell about the sixteen year old boy named Ray, who was paralyzed from the neck down. When I went to the hospital and prayed for him, he was healed and walked out of the hospital the same night! I tell about the kitten that was dying, bleeding from its nose, it's mouth, and it's ears, and unable to move. When I prayed, "In the name of Jesus Christ, rise up and walk!", the bleeding stopped and it immediately jumped up and began leaping all over the yard, totally healed!

David spoke his faith and dismantled the strategy of the enemy, which was to discourage and defeat David. Speaking your faith will dismantle the strategy of the enemy coming against you, as well. Saul immediately gave in and said, "Go and the Lord be with you!"

Saul then clothed David with his own armor, but it wouldn't work for David. It didn't fit him.

He said, "I can't walk with these, for I have not tested them." So David took them off. (I Samuel 17:39)

It's unwise to try to wear the armor of someone else. We must put on our own armor that the Lord has given us and begin to test it in small steps of faith to prepare us for larger steps of faith. David chose five smooth stones from the brook, put them in a pouch he had and, with sling in hand, he drew near to the Philistine. I believe the Lord directed him to do this. It was God's strategy for victory for that occasion. There are different strategies for different occasions. If it was the stone alone that would win the victory, God would have told David to choose a large sharp stone. It was not the stone, but the strategy of God for this victory. The smooth stone must have looked ridiculous, but it often takes the ridiculous to see the miraculous! It's important to hear what God is saying or see what God is doing in each situation and move with him. That's what will bring victory.

How could a kid like David move out so boldly toward a hulk-like monstrous champion like Goliath? He must have looked as foolish as a gnat rushing to attack a lion! What gave him such exorbitant confidence?

David had an intimate relationship with his God and was obedient to Him. He knew that the wonderful promises of God were true and they applied to Him. He had them stored in his heart and meditated on them habitually. Possibly the Lord brought this to his remembrance:

The Lord shall cause your enemies who rise up against you to be defeated before your face; they shall come out against you one way and flee before you seven ways. (Deuteronomy 28:7)

Goliath, with his shield-bearer and his shield in front of him, began moving toward David. When he got a good look at this kid, he underestimated David and he felt David was way beneath him. He despised him and tried to humiliate him. Goliath said to David,

> *"Am I a dog that you come to me with sticks?" He cursed David by his gods. "Come to me, and I will give your flesh to the birds of the air and the beasts of the field!"* (I Samuel 17:43,44)

Just the same way Satan attacks us with lying threats, it was the strategy of the devil through Goliath. Boasting boisterously, his voice resounding across the valley, he tried to intimidate David. Intimidate means to make timid or fearful; to inspire or affect with fear.

This is one of the devil's strongest attacks against us. Every one of us has felt intimidated at some time. If we don't learn to recognize it and take authority over that intimidating spirit in Jesus name, it will keep us suppressed and we'll not fulfill the will of God for our lives. An intimidating spirit says things like, "You're not as good as they are." "You don't have enough power." "If you step out in faith, you'll look foolish!" "If you do that, you'll be humiliated and rejected." An intimidating spirit disguises itself in many ways. It probably will come through someone you respect. Otherwise it would have little effect. So don't react negatively to the person. Possibly he doesn't realize that you are being intimidated. Remember that it is not the person coming against you! It's an intimidating spirit, and you, in the name of Jesus, can take authority over it!

If you don't recognize it, you will be affected by its power, and you will probably end up intimidating someone else. Learn to recognize and identify it!

Our battlefield is our mind. The enemy plants thoughts there. We must quickly recognize their source when they are dropped in, before they take root and grow and become ungodly beliefs in our hearts.

David gave no place in his mind to intimidating words like, "You're too young!" "You're too little!" "You're too inexperienced!" "You're not equipped!" "I'll defeat and kill you!"

> *"And do not (for a moment) be frightened or intimidated in anything by your opponents and adversaries, for such (constancy and fearlessness) will be a clear sign (proof and seal) to them of (their impending) destruction; but (a sure token and evidence) of your deliverance and salvation, and that from God."* (Philippians 1:28 Amplified Bible)

> *David said to Goliath, "You come to me with a sword, with a spear, and with a javelin. But I come to you in the name of the Lord of hosts, the God of the armies of Israel, whom you have defied."* (I Samuel 17:45)

He was saying, "I see all your big powerful weapons, but what I have is much more powerful! It's the name of the Lord! It's in His power and authority and strength I come to you!" David was not representing the army of Israel. He wasn't even qualified by their standards. He was called and anointed by God. He represented the God of the armies of Israel!

We have been given the name of Jesus, which is above every other name! Just as a policeman operates in the name of the law, we must operate in the name of Jesus, in His power and authority! We've been given power of attorney! We're a part of a mighty army! Our commander has never been defeated and never will be and He lives inside of us!

> *For though we walk (live) in the flesh, we are not carrying on our warfare according to the flesh and using mere human weapons. For the weapons of our warfare are not physical {weapons of flesh and blood}, but they are mighty before God for the overthrow and destruction of strongholds."* (II Corinthians 10:3 & 4 Amplified Bible)

Old weapons that we've used in the past will no longer work for us, weapons like persuasion, manipulation, control, charisma, charm, mesmerizing, condemnation, self-pity, intimidation, anger, lies, and deception. Most of us are all too familiar with these weapons. Many of them have been used against us at some time. Many of them have been used by us. We grew up with them and have clung to them like childhood friends. They are not weapons for God's army, but Satan's! It is absolutely imperative that we lay down the weapons that are familiar to us...even comfortable to us. (After all, they've been effective in getting our "way" for years.) Do you want your way or God's? Lay them down!! Refuse to pick them up again so that you can stand in the power of the Lord!

> *Strip yourselves of your former nature (put off and discard your old unrenewed self) which characterized your previous manner of life and becomes corrupt through lusts and desires that spring from delusion; and be constantly renewed in the spirit of your mind (having a fresh mental and spiritual attitude). And put on the new nature (the regenerate self) created in God's image, (Godlike) in true righteousness and holiness."* (Ephesians 4:22-24 Amplified Bible)

Put off implies a total abandoning and casting away, like an old tattered garment never to be put on again. It's relinquishing one's old attitudes and ways of responding. You would look ridiculous if you wore a beautiful brand new silk suit of clothes on top of your old worn-out, frayed and dirty sweat suit. It would not only be uncomfortable, but it would make your new suit look bad. We often make Jesus look bad to others because we've refused to take off the old, and are trying to wear two suits.

Many of us feel stripped bare when we lay down all the weapons that are a part of us. We may feel defenseless, but we are not! It is then we can put on the Lord Jesus Christ. He is then our defense! Now there is room for the mighty presence and power of God to envelop us, to empower us, and we can go forward in the mighty name of Jesus, in His power! In other words, it's as though Jesus Christ Himself is standing there in full power and authority! Who can defeat Him?

Look at how David spoke his faith.

> *"This day the Lord will deliver you into my hand, and I will strike you and take your head from you. And this day I will give the carcasses of the camp of the Philistines to the birds of the air and the wild beasts of the earth, that all the earth may know that there is a God in Israel. Then all this assembly shall know that the Lord does not save with sword and spear; for the battle is the Lord's, and He will give you into our hands."* (I Samuel 17:46-47)

What's the purpose of winning the battle? David's motive is not for his fame or recognition or fortune. What's the cause? So that all the earth will know that there is a God!

David spoke his faith. He didn't allow himself the opportunity to dwell on how big or how mighty his enemy was or how much destruction he had already caused or how much he was capable of causing in the future. He saw God's initiative and he determined in his heart that he would do it, so he began speaking it.

When we are in a battle, we need to speak things like this:

Through God we shall do valiantly, for it is He Who shall tread down our enemies! (Psalm 108:23 and 60:12)

Jesus said, "Behold I give you the authority to trample on serpents and scorpions, and over all the power of the enemy, and nothing shall by any means hurt you." (Luke 10:19)

Hear what God is saying to you about your battle. Proclaim what God says concerning your victory! Speak victory over the situation! Let all the earth know that there's a God! Declare that the weapons of the Lord are more powerful! Declare the battle is the Lord's! Declare that the enemy will be given into our hands!

Now faith is being sure of what we hope for, certain of what we do not see. (Hebrews 11:1)

David had "now faith." He didn't go by what he saw or heard or felt. He perceived as real fact what was not revealed to his senses in any way! He had the assurance that what God had spoken about defeating our enemies and giving us the victory was absolutely true! Our greatest enemies are fear, doubt, and unbelief; fearful of what the enemy will do to us, doubtful of what God will do on our behalf, and unbelief of what God has already told us.

David bragged on God and what He could and would do. He praised God, another important key to victory. When the Israelites asked God who should go up first to win the battle, the Lord said,

"Judah shall go up". (Judges 1:1&2)

Judah means praise. We must go into battle praising God.

So it was, when the Philistine arose and came and drew near to meet David, that David hurried and ran toward the army to meet the Philistine. (I Samuel 17:48)

David didn't run from his enemy, he ran toward him! We need to face our enemies with confidence in our God to defeat them. It is important that when you see the enemy stick up his ugly head, you confront him quickly. I read recently that in Africa, the oldest lion has the loudest roar, but he is also toothless.

Submit yourselves therefore to God. Resist the devil, and he will flee from you. (James 4:7)

Resist doesn't mean "run from." It means: To withstand, to be able to repel. To exert oneself to counteract, to defeat or frustrate. To exert force in opposition. It is extremely important to first submit to God. In His power we can defeat the enemy!

Then David put his hand in his bag and took out a stone; and he slung it and struck the Philistine in his forehead, so that the stone sank into his forehead, and he fell on his face to the earth. (I Samuel 17:49)

With one smooth stone, David struck Goliath, and he fell on his face to the ground. It's important to ask God for His strategy to defeat the enemy! When we follow the strategy the Lord has given us, we also will hit the target and defeat our enemy!

> *For this purpose was the Son of God manifest to destroy the works of the evil one.* (I John 3:8b)

Oftentimes God's strategy will not make sense to our natural minds, but we must seek Him, hear his strategy and follow exactly as He leads to attain victory. The Lord gave very specific instructions at the Battle of Jericho.

> *March around Jericho one time for six days. And seven priests shall bear before the ark seven trumpets of ram's horns; and the seventh day you shall march around the enclosure seven times and the priests shall blow the trumpets. When they make a long blast with the ram's horn, and you hear the sound of the trumpet, all the people shall shout with a great shout, and the wall of the enclosure shall fall down in its place and the people shall go up over it.* (Judges 6:1-5)

There had to be someone in their midst crying, "This is ridiculous! We've never done it this way before!" This strategy would not have found a comfortable place in their natural minds. It certainly didn't seem reasonable. But when God's strategy was followed, it was totally effective! It worked exactly as God had spoken!

God is saying to His army today, "Move out of what is comfortable to your flesh and has satisfied multitudes in the church for centuries. Move into My Spirit. Allow Me to consume you and your natural ways so I can give you victory after victory, that I may receive the glory."

> *So David prevailed over the Philistine with a sling and a stone, and struck the Philistine and killed him. But there was no sword in the hand of David.* (I Samuel 17:50)

The definition of prevail is to conquer or triumph. The victory is not in how many weapons you use nor in how powerful your weapons are. The victory will come through God's strategy. Strategy means the science and art of employing the armed strength of a fighting person (God) to secure the objects of war; the large scale planning and directing of operations in adjustment to combat area, possible enemy action and alignments. God sees the whole picture. He knows the exact strategy to defeat the enemy.

We must learn not to fight battles God has not given us to fight. When we fight God's battles in God's way, at His command, in His power, at His time, we prevail!

> *Yet amid all these things we are more than conquerors and gain a surpassing victory through Him who loves us.* (Romans 8:37)

> *Now thanks be to God Who always leads us in triumph in Christ, and through us diffuses the fragrance of His knowledge in every place.* (2 Corinthians 2:14)

> *Therefore David ran and stood over the Philistine, took his sword and drew it out of its sheath and killed him, and cut off his head with it. And when the Philistines saw that their champion was dead, they fled.* (I Samuel 17:51)

When we aim for the big one, the rest will flee! Aim for the stronghold! Goliath's huge sword was used to cut off his own head!

David's act of courage caused the rest of the Israeli army to rise up and shout and pursue the Philistines, and they plundered their tents. They not only defeated their enemies, but they collected the spoils of war! Your acts of courage, in doing what God calls you to do, will give others around you courage to win victories!

David continued to be prepared to be king. When mighty warrior Saul became jealous of him and wanted him killed, David never responded to Saul's jealousy, anger or hatred. He kept his heart pure and continued to respond to God. He spent time in caves, hiding out from those who would kill him. He had opportunity to kill Saul, but he would not! He waited on God for His time to promote him to his place of destiny, and God did!

Below are listed sixteen important points to remember, in order to live in victory.

REMEMBER THAT GOD HAS GIVEN YOU THE VICTORY!

1. Spend time getting to know your God, through Bible study, prayer, and listening to Him, so that you can be confident that He is not only able, but perfectly willing to deliver you.
2. Recognize your real enemy, his strategies, and his place, which is under your feet.
3. Choose not to be offended.
4. Do not allow discouragement to overtake you. Build up your hope in the Word of God.
5. Remember and rehearse the victories God has already given you.
6. Prophesy victory!
7. Be sure to put on your own armor.
8. Take a step of faith.
9. Do not be intimidated!
10. Go in the name of the Lord and in His power and authority!

11. Declare the battle is the Lord's and it is He who will tread down His enemies!
12. Speak your faith! Speak victory!
13. Don't run from your enemy! Confront your enemy!
14. Lay down your own weapons and fleshly strategy. Tune in to God's strategy for each battle.
15. Ask God to show you the stronghold. Aim for the big enemy! The rest will flee!
16. Remember your victory will give others courage to walk in victory.

CHAPTER SIX

GRUMBLIN' IN THE WILDERNESS OR ENJOYING THE JOURNEY?

Did you ever step into a house where the atmosphere was so thick you could cut it with a knife? Instantly you sense that, before you entered, there was some dissension and strife going on? Possibly there was a lot of grumbling and complaining, releasing much negative energy into the atmosphere. On the other hand, have you stepped into a house where you felt such peace and joy that you never wanted to leave? The atmosphere in the house is determined by the attitudes of the occupants of the house.

On the way to Destiny is a very special place called Wilderness. It's the place where it doesn't seem your prayers are being answered, yet you begin to feel the closeness of God like never before. It's a hard place. It's often a lonely place and may be a very painful place. It's the place where nothing works the way you thought it would. Nothing works the way it used to. But if you press into God during those times, you'll go places in Him that you could not otherwise go.

The devil comes to you, in your place of wilderness, and tells you that you must have missed God or that you have sinned and brought on all the difficulty yourself. There may be some well-meaning friends or relatives who are speaking in agreement with that. If you dwell on their comments, you could get into a lot of confusion, which leads to fear and depression. Then you come to the Valley of Decision. Who will you listen to? Will you believe what God has spoken that seemed to bring you to this place, or will you listen to the words of the devil that will bring more confusion, fear, doubt, and depression? This is the time that you must learn to lean on what God has already spoken, even if you are having difficulty hearing Him at the time. What has He already spoken to you? Stand on that. Speak in agreement with that even if all circumstances are shouting the very opposite.

Wilderness is a necessary part of the journey. I'm not sure I fully understand why, but I do have some insight on the subject. I remember when I was only a few months old in the Lord, I wrote the following song:

> *Spirit of the Living God*
> *Burn in me!*
> *Spirit of the Living God*
> *Burn in me!*
> *Burn out the flesh and dross!*
> *Darkness and sin expose!*
> *Spirit of the Living God*
> *Bur-r-r--n----in me!*

I meant those words with all my heart, but had very little understanding what it would cost. When things began to disappear from my life, it was painful. I remember times of feeling helpless. I tried to do all the right things, and nothing seemed to work.

In August 1978 Dell (my husband, now deceased) and I, along with our two children, had moved to Arizona at the word of the Lord. We were given a vision, which God named, "City on a Hill", and we were very excited about fulfilling it. We had no idea where in Arizona God would plant us, but we went out with a list of places that Dell had methodically compiled and we began driving around from city to city, looking for the right place. We started in the Phoenix area, since his parents lived in Mesa. We then looked at Wickenburg, Flagstaff, and Prescott. We were feeling a little discouraged and then we drove into Lake Havasu City, the last place on the list. I'd never heard of it, nor was I even interested in it, but as we drove from Parker into Lake Havasu City, we saw the clear blue water winding through the beautiful red rock mountains and the view was almost breathtaking! We all felt strongly this was the place. We went home and prepared to move, listing our new two-story colonial home for sale. People asked me, "How can you leave this beautiful home?" I said, "It's easy when you know God is leading."

The little white country church we had been attending, Wheatland Missionary Church, gave us a send-off and my friend Sharon dedicated a song to me. It was *"Learning to Lean."* I was a little offended, thinking I was already leaning on God. "What more is there to learn about leaning?" I had no clue how much more I had to learn about leaning!

I felt we would begin the vision right away after we settled in, but Dell said it would take at least two years before we began. I thought that sounded like a very long time and I exclaimed, "No way!" Through purchasing our new home, Dell was offered a good job as construction supervisor and readily accepted it. I became charter president of Women's Aglow, which I enjoyed tremendously, and all was going very well! I was loving life so much that at times I felt like I needed to pinch myself to be sure it wasn't a dream.

In December of 1979 the economy took a dive and Dell's boss was suddenly selling few houses, so Dell took a voluntary layoff. For three and a half years he was unemployed and could not find a job.

That's when our Wilderness began. It didn't take long to use up our excess money, so we sold our three lots for just what we had paid for them, which was not much. That kept us going financially for a while. We continued praying, seeking God for direction, and waiting on Him. We would sense God's presence very close at times, but He would merely say, "Wait on Me." We stayed involved in church and occasionally we would receive a prophetic word of hope and promise and confirmations to the vision.

Before Dell's job ended, I had kept praying that He would spend time studying God's Word. God answered by removing the job, so he had plenty of time. He began studying the Bible from cover to cover, and the Word was working in his heart. There was a great tenderizing taking place, and he was becoming very compassionate in areas he had not been, prior to that time.

It was a new and challenging experience to have my husband home 24 hours a day, seven days a week, so it gave God the opportunity to work some things out of me as well. The most significant thing God was doing was working on increasing our faith.

Now faith is being sure of what we hope for, certain of what we do not see. (Hebrews 11:1)

Grumblin' In The Wilderness Or Enjoying The Journey?

One thing we were certain of is that we didn't see anything that resembled our vision coming to pass. Any personal resources, that we once had to begin the project, were quickly depleted. We would go up on the foothills above the city at the end of Cherry Tree Boulevard and pray and God would meet us there every time. From that high place, it seemed we could get God's perspective on our situation, as we would prophesy over Lake Havasu City and the whole area. It seemed I could hear God's voice clearer and it would strengthen my faith. I remember one day crying out to God and coming to the mindset that, if all God wanted me to do was minister to people in my daily walk, I would continue doing that and be at peace. I surrendered myself to God in many ways. I surrendered my children to Him at different times. I remember actually laying them on the altar and taking my hands off them, visualizing Him coming and putting His arms around them and taking them for His purposes. Did I do some grumbling when I was in that wilderness? I surely did. There were times when the circumstances seemed overwhelming. One of those grumbling days, I heard this song rise up in my spirit: It's called "Grumblin'."

Are ya grumblin', grumblin' in the wilderness
"Oh, when will this trial end?"
Are ya grumblin', grumblin' in the wilderness
"Oh, when will this trial end?"

Come, My children, stop grumblin' now
Lift your head and look unto Me.
I am well able to deliver you.
When I speak, you'll be set free!

There are lessons to be learned in the wilderness.
Let patience do a work in you.
You will come forth a brand new man.

Faith in Me will bring you through.

Hold fast your confidence in Me
For it'll bring a great reward.
Remember that your anchor is -
In Jesus Christ, your Lord!

God amazingly met our needs and even some desires during that wilderness time! I remember one morning as I was getting dressed for the day, I thought, "I sure wish I had a red blouse." (A menial thing, right?") Later that day a package was delivered to my house. In it was a very pretty brand new red blouse!

Many times I laid the vision on the altar, and told God to kill it if He was not in it. Within 24 hours, He would send someone to confirm the vision once again. One time, moments after laying the vision down, He sent two teenage girls to our door with a picture that symbolized the vision. They had just felt led to purchase it for us.

One time at an Aglow Regional Retreat at Rio Rico Resort, south of Tucson, a lady I had never met came to me and said, "God is saying, "Don't let go of the vision. I see many lights on a hill. Don't let go of the vision." Again a little later she came to me and said, "Don't let go of the vision!"

Over the years, there have been prophecies from other people in ministry, who didn't know me, to confirm the vision.

In the beginning I had been open about sharing the vision with people. At one point a group of people that we fellowshipped with decided to start the vision. They asked us to be a part of it and God said, "Don't touch it. I'm not in it." It was very painful to watch all our church family getting excited about something I wasn't allowed to touch. One Wednesday night the Pastor, who we dearly love, was holding the keys to the Havasu Hotel, which they had just purchased for City On A Hill Annex. (that's what they named their project.) The whole church was praising God for it! I remember coming home from church with my children in the car, crying out to God loudly, "I don't understand!" My daughter, a senior in high school, said, "Mom, you're always saying you want to know Jesus in a deeper way. He's allowing you to experience a little of how He felt at times." Those words penetrated my heart! I knew those words were true and right from God and it quieted my spirit, as I released it all to Him one more time. I have said repeatedly the following is my life scripture:

> *[For my determined purpose is] that I may know Him [that I may progressively become more deeply and intimately acquainted with Him, perceiving and recognizing and understanding the wonders of His Person more strongly and more clearly], and that I may in that same way come to know the power outflowing from His resurrection [which it exerts over believers], and that I may so share His sufferings as to be continually transformed [in spirit into His likeness even] to His death, [in the hope] that if possible I may attain to the [spiritual and moral] resurrection [that lifts me] out from among the dead [even while in the body]* (Philippians 3:10, 11 Amplified Version)

The sufferings spoken of here are persecutions. Whatever it takes for me to die to more of me and be filled with more resurrection life, I say, "yes" to. I declare, "That same Spirit that raised Christ from the dead dwells in me!"

Even the quotes that were on the front page of the newspaper, a few days later, concerning the vision, were my quotes, being spoken by someone else as his own quotes. Our best friend was living with us at the time, and he got involved in the project and worked on it almost every day. That was very painful, but as I would lift up the situation to the Lord, He would again say, "Don't touch it!"

Three months later it came to a halt and the project was stopped. I felt that God said it was an Ishmael before the Isaac. When there is a great promise being birthed, there is often an Ishmael that precedes the fulfillment of the promise. There often will be a mirage that seems so real that it appears to be the real thing! Then, as quickly as it appeared, it disappeared. I have no ill regard or unforgiveness for anyone who took part in it. They're still my friends and I love them. I know that it was my personal test: Would I be so anxious to fulfill the vision that I would run ahead of God to accomplish it? Would I value what all of my friends were saying more than God's Word to me? My answer was "No" on both counts. It was a valuable learning experience for me of the importance of hearing God's voice above every other voice and obeying that voice no matter what it feels like or looks like or how painful or lonely it is. It seemed to deepen and strengthen my relationship with God even more. It's amazing how, out of the deep dark experiences with God, there comes an increase of light and life that you didn't possess previously. So I am thankful for the pain and the trial and my friends who misunderstood.

Out of the pain of all that experience came the following song from the Lord:

I AM THE GREAT I AM

I am the great I Am and I am able.
I am the great I Am and I am able.
I am able to deliver. I am able to save
For I am the great I Am and I am able.

I have called you by My name
And I have bought you.
I have called you by My name

And I have bought you.
I have called you from above
And you are the one I love
I have called you by My name
And I have bought you.

I have done a work in you that shall continue.
I have done a work in you that shall continue.
Hold fast to what you know
And just let My Spirit flow
For I have done a work in you that shall continue.

So just keep your eyes on Me and keep on marching.
Just keep your eyes on Me and keep on marching.
You are in My army now
And your hand is to the plow.
So just keep your eyes on Me and keep on marching.

For I am the great I Am and I am able
I am the great I Am and I am able
I am able to deliver
I am able to save
For I am the great I Am and I am able.

The song brought me hope, peace, and comfort, but most of all, as I heard those words from Him, it brought a personal intimate touch from God that I so desperately needed at that time, in order to be reminded that He knew exactly how I felt and He was right there with me.

When God said He is *"I Am"*, He was saying, *"I am the God Who is actively present with you."* Wow! What an awesome blessing to have the God of Creation actively present beside me and inside of me and all around me and He's working on my behalf! He's gone before me and He's got my back! He's

All Knowing, All Sufficient, All Powerful! He loves me and He cares about everything that concerns me! He knows exactly what it will take to bring me into my destiny!

Another song that the Lord sang to me in the wilderness is the following:

With You

Come walk with Me and take My hand.
I'll take you to the Promised Land
And I'll be with you, with you.
I'll be with you.

When the going gets rough, you feel so alone
Know that I'm there, and you're My own
For I am with you, with you.
I am with you.

When flood waters are high and the fire gets hot
Your friends will be there to say you're not
You're not with Me, with Me!
You're not with Me!

You speak to the fire and tell it to "Go!"
You speak to the flood "Don't overflow!"
I say, "I am with you, with you
I am with you.

On days so cloudy you can't see
And you can't feel the presence of Me
I'll be with you, with you.
I'll be with you

Believe Me, child, press into Me.
I'm purifying you and setting you free
For I am with you, with you
I am with you.

When you've come through the fire so hot
Like precious gold that's worth a lot
They'll know you've been with Me, with Me
They'll know you've been with Me.

The more you have pressed into Jesus in the hard times, the more you'll smell like His sweet fragrance. Others will smell it and be drawn to you. They may ask what it is they are smelling or sensing, thus giving you the opportunity to share the love and faithfulness of Jesus with them.

In November of 1981 we were getting financially desperate. Dell had been trying diligently to find work, reading the want ads and pursuing every opportunity of employment, but the doors seemed to close as fast as they opened. Our checking account balance was down to four dollars and we had no income. We were trying to sell our 1978 Blazer to get some cash.

On a Thursday we received a letter from my nephew Dean who was attending college at Azusa Pacific in California. He said he was coming over for Thanksgiving weekend. I love spending time with Dean, but, because of our circumstances, I instantly thought, "Oh great. I hope he's bringing the turkey."

My thoughts continued in that vein. "Christmas is just around the corner. How will we celebrate with no money for cards or gifts or food?" I was feeling very depressed. I looked around at our beautiful home with cheery yellows and blues and thought, "We have everything we need, except money. No one realizes we're in need because we look like we're doing fine."

I laid down on the yellow and blue floral sofa in the living room and began to cry out to the Lord, "Lord, I feel like I'm in mourning! If You know where I am in this situation, please show me through a long distance phone call." I don't know why I prayed that specifically. I'd never prayed that way before nor have I since.

Friday and Saturday continued to look bleak but on Sunday I began to get unexpected long distance phone calls. The first one was from Dell's sister Jean from Michigan. She said she had just come from church, where an evangelist had been ministering, and she felt to call and tell us what the evangelist had said. I was very encouraged, as she had never done that before.

Next came another call from Michigan from Hollis Sanford, who had attended the same church we had attended when we lived back there. She had never called me before, nor has she ever called me since that day, but that particular day she said she felt led to call and encourage us with some excerpts from the message she had heard that morning in church.

By this point I was getting very encouraged. Then my Mom called from Michigan. That was not unusual as she loved me and called every week or so. However, she was unusually encouraging. This made three long distance phone calls of encouragement. I knew God had heard my prayer!

On Sunday evening my daughter Natalie called from Oral Roberts University in Tulsa, Oklahoma. She was in her second year of college and had no clue what we were experiencing, as we didn't want to burden her. Her opening line was, "Mom, you're not going to believe what happened tonight! I went to the vespers service. I got there a little late, so I had to go way up to the front to find a seat. I sat down by a big black man, and when I did, I felt the anointing of God all over him! Then they introduced him as the speaker, a missionary from the Bahamas, Miles Monroe! He gave a great message and at the end of it he said, 'Now we are going to take communion and I want you to go to someone in the congregation, serve them communion, and make a commitment to them to be their friend and continue to pray for them.' Then Miles came down to me, served me communion, and began to pray for me. Suddenly he began to prophesy, 'and I am going to turn your mother's mourning into joy! And I am going to turn the keys to her vehicle over to the right person. Now call your mother and tell her that.'"

Natalie then asked me, "What's all that about?"

I was crying by then and it took a bit to get myself under control enough to tell her what I had prayed the previous Thursday, "Lord, I feel like I'm in mourning. If you know where I am in this situation, please show me through a long distance phone call."

I was rejoicing! It was so awesome to me that He knew exactly where I was and what I was feeling and what I was saying to Him! He gave me, not just one long distance phone call, but four of them, and the final one was such an awesome confirmation!

The following day, Monday, when the mail arrived, there were four envelopes. The first one I opened was from my nephew Jeff Noble in Michigan. He was a carryout boy at the IGA grocery store and had never before written to me. He wrote a letter saying, "Last night I had a dream and God told me to send you $100.00." In the envelope was a check for $100.00! Wow! How humbling!

The next letter was from the poor little country church in Michigan that had given us the send-off.. The enclosed note stated, "We just felt God wanted us to send you this." In that envelope was $100.00! I had never known them to do anything like that before.

I could hardly wait to open the next envelope! It was from Michigan also from my widowed mom, who was struggling financially herself. There was a check for $100 and a note saying she just felt led to send it to us.

There was one more envelope. It was from our local bank and it had a deposit slip for $100! We had not made any recent deposits, so I called the bank. When the teller answered, I asked her who deposited the money into our account. After checking into it, her answer was, "They wish to remain anonymous." I said, "Ah, I know who it was! It was Jesus of Nazareth!"

Dell and I began praising and worshiping the Lord with all our might, weeping and rejoicing! It became such a reality that our God is not a distant God, who glances at us once in a while, but He's a personal intimate God Who hears our every cry and cares about every detail of our lives. He really will supply all of our needs according to His riches in glory in Christ Jesus, as the Bible says in Philippians 4:19.

From that time on, things began to turn around for us. Soon after, Dell found work. I believe that God allowed us to go through that wilderness experience, so we would begin to fully trust Jehovah Jireh, our Provider, as the God Who Provides. He is our Source and He wants us to expect supernatural provision, as we follow Him.

There were other times the Lord would tell us to go somewhere and there would be no obvious provision to go. If we would just obey and make plans to go, the provision would come. That's different than saying, "If the Lord provides, I will go." It is saying, "Lord, I believe You are saying to go and I trust You will provide. I will make plans to go, trusting You for the provision."

One vitally important thing God wants us to learn is to hear His voice and have an obedient heart. Many times you must put action to your obedience. Faith without works is dead. That's not talking about our own works, but what the Father shows us to do. Even Jesus said, *"My food is to do the will of the Father Who sent me, and to finish His work."* (John 4:34)

Grumblin' In The Wilderness Or Enjoying The Journey?

Another song I received in 1982 is the following:

I'm not ruled by the rain.
I'm not ruled by the snow.
I'm not ruled by this place
Or any place I go.

I'm not ruled by other people.
I'm not ruled by what they say.
I only serve my Father
Every day!

I'm not ruled by my finances.
I'm not ruled by my needs
I'm not ruled by other spirits
Or the negative thoughts they feed.

I'm just standing on the Word of God.
I live in victory!
I'm ruled by the Holy Spirit
And He sets me free!

CHAPTER SEVEN

DYING TO LIVE

In order to rebuild a house, first some things have to go. You have to die to your attachment to those things you have felt comfortable with all those years. Those old things will only cause deterioration and will destroy the effects of the new house, the new look, and the new life.

"I'm dying to see that movie!" "I'm dying to wear that dress!" We've all heard expressions like these. We could say, "I'm dying to go to heaven!" and we would be correct. That's normally how people get there. (a little humor) In kingdom language, "I'm dying to live!" is accurate, because there is no resurrection where there is no death. Most of us want resurrection power in our lives. It requires death to self. As a young Christian I grabbed onto Romans 6:11: *Reckon yourselves dead to sin and alive unto God.* I would say, "Dead to self! Alive unto God in Christ Jesus!" It would bring into alignment my perspective and remind me that the old me died on the cross, and now Jesus lives in me and through me! We need to stop trying to fix the old man! See him nailed to the cross and then buried in the grave. See Jesus in you coming forth from the grave in resurrection power!

That reminds me of another song the Lord gave me in my early years of following Him:

I'm dead to sin (clap, clap, clap, clap)
But I'm ali-i-ive unto God in Christ Jesus!
I'm dead to sin, (clap, clap, clap, clap)
But I'm ali-i-ive unto God in Christ Jesus!

The old me died upon that cross
Was buried in that tomb
A new me rose again with Christ
Now His life is in my womb!

Singing that has brought me victory again and again! That's amazing to me! Only in Christianity does death bring life!

I have been crucified with Christ; it is no longer I who live, but Christ lives in me; and the life, which I now live in the flesh I live by faith in the Son of God, Who loved me and gave Himself for me. (Galatians 2:20)

Jesus represented me on the cross. He represented me in the grave. He represented me when He rose from the dead in resurrection power. He represented me when He was seated in heavenly places. It was all about me when He left His place in Heaven and came to earth as a baby. He didn't need to do it for Himself. He needed to do it for you and me. We were hopeless without Him and heading for Hell, as Adam had sold us out to the enemy camp. Someone had to pay the price to buy us back. It had to be a sinless one. Only Jesus could do it.

Whoa! I just got a revelation! If Jesus represented me on the cross, in the grave, and in the resurrection and ascension into heaven, couldn't it be that He represented me when He went into Hell and took back from Satan the keys of Hell and death? (I think I just experienced a fresh surge of power and authority!)

> *He said, "I give you the keys to the kingdom".* (Matthew 16:19)

What are keys for? Unlocking or gaining access into a place that was locked. We now have the power to access heaven and come boldly before the throne of God! We now have power to bind and to loose. He repeats it again when He says,

> *"Assuredly I say to you, "whatever you bind on earth will be bound in heaven, and whatever you loose on earth will be loosed in heaven. Again! I say to you that if two of you agree on earth concerning anything that they ask, it will be done for them by My Father in heaven."* (Matthew 18:18,19)

What does that mean? The word bind means to put in bonds, to confine, restrict, restrain, to constrain with legal authority, to wrap around. The word loose means to break up, destroy, unbind, release, to let loose, to free from confinement, and restrain. Jesus is saying that we now have power to forbid on earth whatever is already forbidden in heaven and we have power to loose or free or release on earth what is already released in heaven. We're to pray, "Your kingdom come, Lord, right where we are, Your will be done here as it is in heaven!" Jesus told us to pray that way, so would He tell us to do something that is not possible? Of course, not!

What are we doing with the keys? Car keys won't unlock the car unless you pick them up, either push the button or put them in the keyhole. Then you need to put them in the ignition and turn on the car, put it in gear, and step on the accelerator. Now you've activated the car.

So there is a process to the keys being effective and the kingdom being activated. First of all, we must study the Bible and spend time in God's presence to learn what the kingdom is like and what heaven is like. We must ask God what He is doing in each situation and speak and act in agreement with Him and what He is doing. Speak those things over places and people and situations. That activates the kingdom of heaven on earth.

Recently this song rose up from my spirit:

Heaven is a comin' to earth today!
Heaven is a comin' to earth!
Heaven is a comin' to earth today!
Heaven is a comin' to earth! Oh, ya!
Heaven is a comin' to earth!

Step aside and let His Spirit flow!
Step aside and let Him move!
Step aside and let His Spirit flow!
Step aside and let Him move!
'Cause

Heaven is a comin' to earth today!
Heaven is a comin' to earth!
Heaven is a comin' to earth today!
Heaven is a comin' to earth! Oh, ya!
Heaven is a comin' to earth!

It's a prophetic song, which releases expectancy for heaven to invade your circumstances and encounters for that day.

> *You were buried with Him in baptism, in which you also were raised with Him through faith in the working of God, who raised Him from the dead. And you, being dead*

> *in your trespasses and the uncircumcision of your flesh, He has made alive together with Him, having forgiven you all trespasses, having wiped out the handwriting of requirements that was against us, which was contrary to us. And He has taken it out of the way, having nailed it to the cross. Having disarmed principalities and powers, He made a public spectacle of them, triumphing over them in it.* (Colossians 2:12-15)

Disarmed means deprived of means of attack, made harmless. Principalities are beings that exercise rule. Powers would be demonic powers. This is saying that Jesus already deprived of the means of attack and made harmless the demonic powers and principalities! We have been given power over them!

> *If then you were raised with Christ, seek those things, which are above where Christ is, sitting at the right hand of God. Set your mind on things above, not on things on the earth. For you died, and your life is hidden with Christ in God.* (Colossians 3:1-3)

Here's a song I received in March 1983:

> *Set your affections on the things above*
> *Not on the things of earth!*
> *Set your affections on the things above*
> *Not on the things of earth!*
> *For you are dead (clap, clap, clap)*
> *And your life is hidden with Chri-i-ist in God!*
> *For you are dead (clap, clap, clap)*
> *And your life is hidden with Chr-i-ist in God!*
>
> *For where your treasure is*
> *There will your heart be also!*

For where your treasure is
There will your heart be also!

Again, my victory is in seeing my old self dead on the cross, dead to attention- getting, selfishness, rejection, and control. Dead to the desire to be first or best or popular! See that old person buried in the tomb, and visualize Jesus coming forth in me and through me in His power, love, and glory! I have been completely cleansed by the blood Jesus shed on the cross! I have been made brand new!

> *Therefore if anyone is in Christ, he is a new creation; old things have passed away, behold, all things have become new.* (II Corinthians 5:17)

I have a brand new identity and a new beginning! I have a brand new image, the one I was intended to have! It's the image of Christ!

> *Then God said, "Let Us make man in Our image, according to Our likeness, let them have dominion over the fish of the sea, over the birds of the air, and over the cattle, over all the earth and over every creeping thing that creeps on the earth. So God created man in His own image; in the image of God He created him; male and female He created them.* (Genesis 1:26, 27)

An earthly king will often have images of himself made in stone or wood or gold or bronze. He then wants these images displayed all over the land to declare to that land that he is king and he has the power & authority over that land and everyone should worship him. Nebuchadnezzar, in the book of Daniel, is a prime example of that.

God is such an awesome king! He created men and women in the image of God, according to the likeness of the Father, Son, and Holy Spirit. Image means likeness, a representation. Image refers to qualities, like personality, intellect, character, and heart. You were created to love like God, sound like God, and act like God. He created you a spirit. You live in a fleshly body, and you have a soul (mind, will and emotions). We were created in His image and then placed all over the world to declare to the world that He is king and to manifest to the world His power, His love, and His authority! He has given it to us! We are His images! We delight in releasing His image and glory in ways that cause people to worship our God.

Through the sin of Adam, man's spirit man died, and our ability to relate to God as our Father died. However, God's love for us is so awesome that He sent Jesus to pay the penalty for that sin and the sins of the world, and by accepting His blood sacrifice, we are restored to that image of God.

Jesus is the image of the invisible God, the firstborn over all creation. (Colossians 1:15)

Selah! Pause here and think about that! Jesus is the image of the invisible God. He is the firstborn of all of us who are to be the image of the invisible God!

Since asking Jesus to come into my heart and take over my life, I'm not the same person anymore. I'm not the timid fearful woman I was once. That woman was nailed to the cross and buried in a tomb. Every sin and every hindrance that stood between my Father God and me has been put to death on the cross and washed away by the blood of Jesus! I've been born again, recreated in the image of God!

Jesus said, "Most assuredly, I say to you, unless one is born again, he cannot see the kingdom of God." (John 3:3)

I couldn't see the kingdom of God before I was born again, but now I have a new capacity to relate, to hear, to see and to speak. My spiritual eyes have been opened! My spiritual ears have been opened! There has been a great awakening in me! I am now a part of the kingdom of God!

Since I have been raised with Jesus and seated in heavenly places, I have a new perspective on things. I can look down at the circumstances with God's perspective.

I have a new mindset, as I now have access to the mind of Christ.

But we have the mind of Christ. (1 Corinthians 2:16)

Then God blessed them, and God said to them, "Be fruitful and multiply; fill the earth and subdue it; have dominion over the fish of the sea, over the birds of the air, and over every living thing that moves on the earth. (Genesis 1:28)

We were created to have relationship with God and worship Him. We're to be fruitful and multiply. In other words, we are to produce more fruit in His image, in His likeness, like Him! We have new authority! We are to subdue the rest of creation, including aggressive satanic forces! Our ability to sustain that role as delegated ruler of the earth will depend upon our continual obedience to God's rule as King of all. It also depends upon our submission to the earthly authorities God has placed over us. When I am submissive to my husband and to the law of the land, I have more power and authority over demonic entities. Rebellion is the beginning of witchcraft, so it will be a huge hindrance to one having spiritual authority.

Jesus said, "Behold, I give you the authority to trample on serpents and scorpions, and over all the power of the enemy, and nothing shall by any means hurt you." (Luke 10:19)

That is a powerful word. One day in 1994, after my husband had passed away, I was living by myself, and I had overslept. I hurriedly dressed and ran off to work, leaving my bed unmade, which was very unusual for me. That night I came home exhausted and crawled into bed. I immediately felt something bite my back. I jumped out of bed and looked to see what had bitten me. It was a scorpion! I grabbed a book off the bedside table and hit it until I felt it was dead. I thought I should save it so that, in case I had to go to the hospital, I could take it with me. I went to the garage, got a coffee can, and scooped the scorpion into it. I then called the hospital and was told to call Poison Control. When I did, the lady who answered the phone said, "Wash the area of your body where you were bitten. Numbness may start in any part of your body, not necessarily in the area where you were bitten. If you do start to go numb, get to the hospital as quickly as you can."

I thought, "Oh, great! I live by myself and, if my head goes numb, I'll drive myself to the hospital? I'd better come up with a better plan." Then the above scripture came to mind. I jumped up and began quoting Luke 10:19 and confessing that I had authority over scorpions and nothing was going to harm me! Then I washed off the area of the bite and went to bed and fell asleep. I had no ill effects from that bite. It pays to know the Word of God, so God can bring it to our minds at just the right moment, and we can stand and take the authority we have been given!

> *Jesus said, "All authority has been given to Me in heaven and on earth. Go therefore and make disciples of all nations, baptizing them in the name of the Father and of the Son and of the Holy Spirit, teaching them to observe all things that I have commanded you, and lo, I am with you always, even to the end of the age." (Mt. 28:18-20)*

What was he saying there? He has all authority. He has told us to go in His authority! By manifesting His love, power and glory, we're to reproduce others in the image of God, who will be baptized into the Father, Son and Holy Spirit. Others, who will die to themselves and be recreated in the image of God, will go and multiply themselves until we fill the earth with the image of God, with His love, His power, and His glory! What an awesome plan! He promises to be with us until the end of the age!

CHAPTER EIGHT

ONENESS

If you had fifty different designers to draw up the plan for your house, how do you think it would turn out? If each one designed a unique room, allowing no thought of how it would flow with the next room, you would just end up with a conglomeration of nice rooms without an overall beautiful presentation and flow, There is only One Designer for your house, just as there is only one Designer for the kingdom of God. We each have a unique part in the plan, and as we all come to Him and seek Him for His vision and His plan, though the individual vision and plan varies, we will all be in agreement. We will all be one. There will be a flowing together which will present to the world the beauty and creativity and awesomeness of our God, which will indeed draw all men to Him.

When Jesus was asked, *"Which is the first commandment of all?"* Jesus quoted from Deuteronomy 6:4 and 5 and answered,

> *The first of all the commandments is: Hear, O Israel, the Lord our God, the Lord is one. And you shall love the Lord your God with all your heart, with all your soul, with all*

your mind, and with all your strength. This is the first commandment. (Mark 12:29 & 30)

Hear, O Israel, the Lord our God; the Lord is one. I've been told by Hebrew scholars that this is confessed daily in Judaism and it is the highest prayer. It is customary to stand as they recite it. What is normally missed in this passage is the importance of the words *hear* and *one*. I've already addressed the importance of hearing in lesson two. What we'll address now is the importance of one. One is the Hebrew word *'echad*. It means one, a unit, united, unity. The root word *'achad* means *to bring together, to unify, to collect one's thoughts*.

We seem to have little comprehension of oneness, but it is so on the heart of God. God is One; yet He is Father, Son, and Holy Spirit. When He created man, He said, "Let Us make man in Our image." Father, Son, and Holy Spirit were involved in creation. The words *Us* and Our were used. The Three in One flowed together in harmony and unity. There was no distinguishing who did what part. Not one received more glory than the other. We were created spirit beings, possessing a soul and living in a body. It is God's desire that those three elements also flow together as one.

We are to be God's image bearers, having the heart of the Father and ruling over the earth. We see a vivid picture of the heart of the Father through Jesus. He and the Father share the same purpose, plan, and power. Knowing that He would soon die on the cross, a cruel death, Jesus set His mind on glorifying the Father. He prayed, *"Glorify Your Son, that Your Son also may glorify You."* (John 17:1)

Eternal life is knowing the Father as the only true God and knowing Jesus. We often have a distorted impression of Who the Father really is, based on our imperfect earthly father or other authority figures. Father God never has an impure or ulterior motive for showing love to us. His agape love is not based on our actions or attitudes. It's not based on how good we are or the good works we have done. It's not based on what we are doing or not doing. He just loves us and wants to be in relationship with us. It gives Him pleasure when we receive His love. He created a garden for us to walk and talk with Him. Though man was evicted from that garden because of sin, Jesus paid the price and penalty for our sin, that we would be restored to that place of relationship with Him.

Jesus came to earth to teach us and demonstrate to us how a relationship with the Father should be. He glorified the Father on the earth by finishing the work the Father gave Him to do. He glorified the Father by making Him known and by leaving a favorable impression or opinion of the Father everywhere He went. We are given an assignment to do the same. We have been called, chosen, appointed, and anointed to do specific assignments. In all of these, we are to demonstrate the power, love, grace, and character of our Father. Jesus manifested the name of Yahweh to mankind. Yahweh, the God Who is actively present, was visualized by those who saw Jesus. Jesus said,

> *"All things which You have given Me are from You and I have given to them the words which You have given Me. They have received them, and have known surely that I came forth from You; and they have believed that You sent Me."* (John 17:7 & 8)

He is saying that because He loved and acted from the heart of the Father, others believed that the Father had sent Him. He caught the initiatives of heaven and did them and it caused people to believe. He has given us what the Father gave Him so that people will surely know we come from Him! We have the same power and authority to operate from the heart of the Father as Jesus did, so that people will know God sent us.

"And all Mine are Yours, and Yours are Mine, and I am glorified in them." (John 17:10)

Now here's a concept that we need to grasp. Help us, Lord! It's not about how many came to the altar in my church or how many sheep I keep in the pen at my church. It's about working together to expand the kingdom of God, where He is King! Each has a part. Each knows in part. We need each other! Pride in individual churches must come down in Jesus name! We need to repent of our foolish pride and competition, and grab hands, and put together our parts to make a whole. We'll see God move in amazing power! I went to a citywide Christian meeting recently where many churches were involved. Some ignored all the rest and cheered loudly for their church's performance. When that part was done, they disappeared. It grieved the Holy Spirit in me, as I could hear His cry, "that we be one as Jesus and the Father are one." That includes honoring and respecting each other, learning from each other, supporting each other, hearing from each other, praying for each other, and flowing together in the power of the Holy Spirit as one body! What a powerful revival could be released through real oneness!

I had a dream a few years ago that I was on a ship. I was expecting multiple births. My son Paul and daughter-in-law Karina were on the ship and Karina also was expecting multiple births. The birthing began and, one after another, the babies were born. We all loved each of them with the same great love. There was no pride of ownership. We were all delighted with all of them! After a while, I thought we were both finished. Then I heard, "Oh, not yet! There's one more coming! Just one more push!" Sure enough! With very little effort, I gave birth to one more baby and she had a lot of dark hair on her head. I asked the Lord, "What's with all the hair? What does that mean?" He said, "The hair represents the glory. Great glory will come forth!" As we flow together as a team, each using his or her gifting, talents, and abilities and acting on the initiatives of heaven, instead of competing or taking personal credit for any of the results, we will see the outpouring of great glory in our cities, regions, and nations! The greatest glory will come at the end of that.

Jesus went on to say that He was leaving and He prayed,

"Keep through Your name those whom You have given Me, that they may be one, as We are." (John 17:11)

The power to keep us safe is in His name! It's not about our name! The keeping power is in whose name? It's in the name of the Lord. The name of the Lord is Yahweh, the God Who is actively present with you. Yahweh Rapha is the God Who is actively present with you, Who heals. He is Yahweh Shammah, the God Who is actively present with you, Who is there.

He is Yahweh Nissi, the God Who is actively present with you, Who is your banner. The banner is the rallying point for troops or announcement of a victory already won. It's a mark of identification.

His banner over me is love. (Solomon 2:4)

Declare His banner is flying over you, announcing His victory that is already won!

He is Yahweh Jireh, the God Who is actively present with you, Who will provide all of your needs. God called Abram to leave his country and his family and go to a land that God promised to show him. He promised to bless Him and make of him a great nation and in him to bless all the families of the earth. God made covenant with Abram and promised him he would have an heir, even though he was already very old. He told him his descendants would be in number as the stars.

Abraham believed in the Lord, and He counted it to him for righteousness. (Genesis 15:6)

God told Abraham to bring a three-year-old heifer, a three-year-old female goat, a three-year-old ram, a turtledove, and a young pigeon to him. He cut each one in two, except for the birds. When it was dark, a smoking oven and a burning torch appeared and passed between those pieces and God made covenant with Abram. God came and walked between the bleeding pieces and took an oath of loyalty to Abram, which was unconditional. God and Abram were irrevocably bound together in blood. The two had become one.

After Abram and Sarai tried to help God out in bringing forth a child through their servant Hagar, because it seemed like such an impossibility that two very old people would have a child, the Lord appeared to Abram, who was then ninety-nine years old, and said,

> *"I am Almighty God; walk before me and be blameless, and I will make My covenant between Me and you, and will multiply you exceedingly."* (Genesis 17:1b)

Then Abram fell on his face, which was the correct reaction. Then God talked with him, saying,

> *"As for Me, Behold, My covenant is with you, and you shall be a father of many nations. No longer shall your name be Abram, but your name shall be Abraham; for I have made you a father of many nations. I will make you exceedingly fruitful and I will make nations of you, and kings shall come from you. And I will establish My covenant between Me and you and your descendants after you in their generations, for an everlasting covenant, to be God to you and your descendants after you."* (Genesis 17:1-7)

God said, *"As for Me"*. He was saying, "I'll make it happen. It's not up to you how that vision comes to pass; it's up to Me to make it happen. You can count on Me to make it happen." He changed Abram's name to Abraham, so that every time he heard his name, he would hear the promise that he would be a father of many nations. God promised them all the land of Canaan, as an everlasting possession and He promised to be their God. He said, *"I will be their God."*

Then God told Abraham what his part would be.

"As for you, you shall keep My covenant, you and your descendants after you: Every male child among you shall be circumcised. (Genesis 17:9,10)

The shedding of blood was a sign of the covenant. The cutting away of the foreskin represented the cutting away of fleshly dependence and demonstrated that their future did not depend on their own ability and what they could do in the flesh. They were making a statement that their confidence was being placed in the promise of God and His faithfulness rather than their own flesh.

When Abraham was 100 years old, he and Sarah had their child of promise, Isaac. When Isaac was a young boy, God tested Abraham and told him to take his only son and offer him as a burnt offering on a particular mountain, which was the same place where God sacrificed His own Son.

Who among us would not have questioned, "God, what are you doing? You gave me a promise and now you are asking me to give up the only means I have of fulfilling the promise. What are you thinking?"

But Abraham rose up early in the morning, took two young men with him, took Isaac his son, and took wood for the burnt offering, and went to the place God told him to go.

It took him three days. Abraham told the young men to stay with the donkey and said,

> "The lad and I will go yonder and worship; and we will come back to you." (Genesis 22:5)

Abraham spoke his faith when he said, "We will come back to you." His confidence was in God. It didn't make sense to the natural mind, but He chose to trust God, so he took the wood, the fire and a knife and the two went up the mountain. Isaac asked his father,

> "Look, the fire and the wood, but where is the lamb for a burnt offering?" (Genesis 22:7)

> Look at Abraham's answer. "My son, God will provide for Himself the lamb for a burn offering." (Genesis 22:8)

When they got to the place God had told Abraham to go, he prepared the altar, placed his son on the altar, and took the knife in his hand. Just then the Angel of the Lord called to him from heaven and told him not to do anything to Isaac.

> God said, "Now I know that you fear God, since you have not withheld your son, your only son, from Me." (Genesis 22:12)

Abraham looked up and there was a ram caught in a thicket by its horns. So Abraham took the ram and offered it up instead of his son. Then Abraham called the name of the place, *"The Lord Will Provide"*. To this day it is said, *"In the Mount of the Lord it shall be provided."* That's the same place where Jesus was offered up, a sacrifice for us, and everything we need is provided through accepting His sacrifice for us.

In 1994 when I was recently widowed, we were entering the Passover season. God spoke to me to have a dinner for city prayer intercessors, followed by a prayer meeting where we were to go to different places in the city and pray. He told me to have lamb for the dinner. I had never cooked one in my life and financially I was not in a position to buy one, but the urging did not let up, so I began to plan the dinner and invite the people. I talked to a caterer in the church named Peggy, about how to cook the lamb. She said she would cook it and I told her I would pay for it. After the dinner, when I approached her to pay for it, she said she could not accept any payment for it. Again, God provided Himself a lamb! It spoke volumes to me about just doing what He says to do and He will provide whatever is needed.

He is Yahweh Shalom; the God Who is actively present with me Who is my peace, my total well-being. Shalom means wholeness, health, prosperity, safety, completeness, and total well-being. Jesus is the Prince of Peace. He said,

> *"These things I have spoken to you, that in Me you may have peace."* (John 16:33)

In Jesus, we have everything we need!

He is Yahweh Tsidkenu, the God Who is actively present with me, Who is my righteousness. My righteousness is as filthy rags. He became sin for me that I would become the righteousness of God in Christ Jesus.

> *For He made Him Who knew no sin to be sin for us, that we might become the righteousness of God in Him.* (II Corinthians 5:21)

He is Yahweh Sabaoth, the God Who is actively present with me, Who is the Lord of armies! No one can defeat Him!! The enemies of the Israeli armies have seen angels fighting with them. We can pray to God, Who is so magnificent and so powerful that all creation serves His purposes!

He is El Roi, the God Who sees. Nothing is hidden from God! As He told Moses at the burning bush,

> *"I have surely seen the oppression of My people who are in Egypt, and have heard their cry because of their taskmasters, for I know their sorrows.* (Exodus 3:7)

Whatever you are encountering at this time, God has not missed it. He knows and He cares and, in His perfect timing, He will fix it. He will bring divine order to every situation. As we lean into Him, and praise Him and worship Him for Who He is, our praise will change the atmosphere around us. Our place of helplessness and hopelessness will be transformed into a place of faith and expectation. Praise Him that He knows your situation. Praise Him that He sees all! Praise Him that His life and light is transforming!

> In John 17:13, *Jesus said, "These things I speak in the world, that they may have My joy fulfilled in themselves."*

This makes me want to speak what He has spoken, so that His joy will be fulfilled in me. He told us we are not of this world, just as He was not of this world. As the Father sent Jesus into the world, He also sent us into the world. How did God send Him? With the power of the Holy Spirit! We can have that same power for the asking. Not in our own strength, but in the power of the Holy Spirit, we can transform the world around us, just as He did! We are to manifest the life of God, the power of God, the love of God and the works of God to the world around us so they will know that He is alive!

> *Jesus said, "I do not pray for these alone, but also for those who will believe in Me through their word; that they all may be one, as You, Father, are in Me, and I in You; that they may be one in Us, that the world may believe that You sent Me."* (John 17:20,21)

Jesus prayed for you and me! He prayed that we all would be one as Jesus and the Father are one! That's how the world will believe that God sent Jesus. That's also how the world will know that God has sent us. He was not talking about just unity within each church building. That is too small-minded for God. He's talking about His body of believers, all of us! He desires that each of us use our gifts and abilities and function together with one mind and one purpose, increasing God's kingdom on the earth.

> *"And the glory which You gave Me I have given them, that they may be one just as We are one: I in them and You in Me; that they may be made perfect in one, and that the world may know that You have sent Me, and have loved them as You have loved Me."* (John 17:22,23)

His presence and His glory resides in us that we may be one just as the Father and Jesus are one! It's the miracle of oneness that only time spent in the presence of the Father can bring! Time spent drinking in of His love and eating at His table of provision, soaking in and being fulfilled by His presence and His personal intimate love will transform us and prepare us to go out and deposit Him and His life into others. The world is looking for change. Let us be the ones who will demonstrate the life change that can happen in God's wonderful presence, and the completeness experienced as we flow together as one body! Let us transform our world!

Pride in only our little part of the body promotes a judgmental spirit and a spirit of competition and comparison. God only has one body. He only has one army. There are many companies within the army, but we have the same commander and every soldier is significant. Pride causes us to be walled off in areas of our life and to other parts of the body. This leads us to the second commandment Jesus gave.

> *And the second, like it, is this: You shall love your neighbor as yourself. There is no other commandment greater that these.* (Mark 12:31)

This one can't happen without doing the first commandment. Hear God. Be one with Him. Allow Him to expose parts of your heart, your soul, your mind, and your strength that are not surrendered to Him. Invite Jesus into those places. Ask Him to show you what is there. Allow Him to heal and restore and make you wholehearted.

> *Therefore you shall be perfect, just as your Father in heaven is perfect.* (Matthew 5:48)

Perfect, in this verse, means openhearted. Aren't you glad our Father is not walled off to us? How openhearted our Father is! I want to be just like Him, don't you?

> *Having been born again, not of corruptible seed but incorruptible, through the word of God which lives and abides forever.* (I Peter 1:23)

I was meditating on that verse years ago, and I realized that I am not of the seed of my earthly father anymore. I am of the seed of my Heavenly Father. This song arose:

Oneness

The seed of my Father is growing in me
Growing in me, growing in me
The seed of my Father is growing in me
And one day like Him I will be!

CHAPTER NINE

KINGDOM MINDSET

The heart of the house God is building is naturally the one that is after the heart of the Father. To have the heart of the Father is to have a kingdom mindset. John the Baptist preached,

> *"Repent, for the kingdom of heaven is at hand!"* (Matthew 3:2)

Repent means, "Make a decision that results in a change of mind, which in turn leads to a change of purpose and action." So, it means, turn around from the way you were walking, thinking, feeling, and operating, in emptiness, darkness, and fruitlessness. Walk in the light and life of Jesus. The kingdom is as close as your hand.

Jesus also began preaching,

> *"Repent, for the kingdom of heaven is at hand."* (Matthew 4:17)

He was saying, "Change your mindset. The kingdom of heaven is as close as your hand." (The kingdom of God and the kingdom of heaven are interchangeable.) God's kingdom was His theme. He was saying, "God is King and beginning right now, we're under God's government."

The first be-attitude is,

> *"Blessed are the poor in spirit, for theirs is the kingdom of heaven."* (Matthew 5:3)

This is the basis for kingdom living. The word blessed in the be-attitudes means large, or of long duration blessings, supremely blessed, a condition in which congratulations are in order. It means to be fully satisfied. This be-attitude implies that the first thing we need to do is recognize our need for a Savior. Recognize and admit that, without Him, we are lacking and needy. Invite Jesus into your lives to set up His kingdom, where He rules and reigns in power. In other words, ask forgiveness for running your own life and doing everything your way, and invite Jesus to come and be king of your life. We can't access heaven without Jesus.

> *Jesus said, "Most assuredly I say to you, unless one is born again, he cannot see the kingdom of God."* (John 3:3)

You'll never be able to recognize the kingdom of God or access it unless you are born again. Once you are born again, you will be able to see and experience the kingdom of God! Spiritual life and relationship with God begin at that point! Your spiritual eyes and spiritual ears are then opened! Your whole being is opened up to the supernatural dimension!

Jesus went on to say,

> *"Most assuredly, I say to you, unless one is born of water and the Spirit, he cannot enter the kingdom of God. That which*

is born of the flesh is flesh, and that which is born of the Spirit is spirit. Do not marvel that I said to you, you must be born again." (John 3:5-7)

Step out of the kingdom of darkness and into the kingdom of God. Submit to the Lordship of Jesus Christ. Allow Him to teach you and mold you into His image. Change your mindset, which is what your mind is set upon, concerning yourself, others, and God. Repent and turn from the judgments you have made concerning yourself, others or God. Allow the Holy Spirit to guide and direct you. Surrender your life, your plans, your attitudes, your ways, and your way of thinking and connect with heavenly thinking.

Those things birthed in the flesh will not produce life, but only that which is birthed of the Spirit realm.

The second be-attitude Jesus spoke was,

"Blessed are those who mourn for they shall be comforted." (Matthew 5:4)

Mourn represents sorrow for our sins and sorrow for the sins of others, in intercession.

God will bless us, comfort us and empower us to pray for others in areas that we have repented of, and from which we have been set free.

The third be-attitude Jesus spoke is,

"Blessed are the meek, for they shall inherit the earth." (Matthew 5:5)

Meek does not mean weak, but power under perfect control of the Holy Spirit. People assume that when a person is meek, it's because he is helpless and cannot help himself. Jesus could have wiped out all the bad guys on the earth, but He didn't. Even though He had access to all the powers of heaven, He was perfectly submitted to His Heavenly Father. Jesus relied on the power of God, the wisdom of God, the will of God, and the timing of God. Meekness is the temper of spirit in which we accept God's dealings with us as good, and, therefore, without complaining or resisting. Meekness combines humility, gentleness, and consideration for others. It is the opposite of self-assertiveness and self-interest; it's the spirit that is neither elevated in superiority or cast down in self-abasement or inferiority. Meekness is the opposite of the world's concept of coveting and grabbing for ourselves whatever we can get. Coveting is lusting after material wealth or position that is outside the plan of God for you. Surrender to God's plan and position brings triumph over the covetous spirit. By being meek, we'll receive the inheritance God has for us.

The fourth be-attitude is,

"Blessed are those who hunger and thirst for righteousness, for they shall be filled." (Matthew 5:6)

Having a passion for God and for the things of God guarantees that you will be fulfilled. What are you most hungry for? It's wise to pray frequently, "Holy Spirit, come shine Your light into my heart, exposing those things that don't line up with your righteousness. I want to be filled with You totally." Spend time at His table, eating the food He provides, studying His Word, drinking in of the Holy Spirit, until you're filled to overflowing, resting in His presence, listening to Him.

The fifth be-attitude is,

"Blessed are the merciful, for they shall obtain mercy." (Matthew 5:7)

Isn't that amazing? We must first receive God's mercy before we can give mercy to others. Then, as we show mercy to others, we obtain more mercy. Doing things God's way always brings an increase. Mercy is showing compassion even when you don't feel people deserve it. It helps to remember we didn't deserve God's mercy; yet He showed it to us in abundance. Mercy combines tendencies with action. Look for ways to manifest God's mercy. He has a way of placing you in circumstances where you have to draw upon God's mercy to feel any compassion toward a person. Then you have the privilege of displaying that mercy. Mercy must be joined with truth; otherwise you have "sloppy agape."

By mercy and truth iniquity is destroyed. (Proverbs 16:6, 20:28, 3:3)

The sixth be-attitude is,

"Blessed are the pure in heart, for they shall see God." (Matthew 5:8)

The devil tries to clog up our hearts with sin and negativity so that we won't see God and be able to follow Him. Fear, doubt, and unbelief will stop the flow of God. Hurt, anger, unforgiveness, pride, and arrogance will also block the word of God from being heard and understood. If we'll be quick to ask forgiveness and receive it, we'll keep a pure heart and be in the flow of what God is doing. Many people check their blood pressure daily, checking the physical life-flow to and from their hearts. We would do well to check the spiritual life-flow to and from our hearts. What is going in? What is coming out?

Out of the abundance of the heart, the mouth speaks. (Matthew. 12:34)

The seventh be-attitude is

> *"Blessed are the peacemakers, for they shall be called sons of God."* (Matthew 5:9)

Jesus is the Prince of Peace. If He lives in us and we abide in Him, He'll empower us to give up our right to be right and to walk in peace. Then the God of Peace will crush Satan under our feet shortly. Let's allow the God of peace to consume us. Then no matter where we go, no matter what the strife-filled circumstances, The God of Peace will crush Satan under our feet! People will recognize and call us sons of God.

The eighth be-attitude is:

> *"Blessed are those who are persecuted for righteousness' sake, for theirs is the kingdom of heaven. Blessed are you when they ridicule and insult and persecute you, and say all kinds of evil against you falsely for My sake. Rejoice and be exceedingly glad, for great is your reward in heaven for so they persecuted the prophets who were before you.* (Matthew 5:10-12)

Notice it clearly states, for righteousness' sake, in contrast to your own foolishness and doing your own thing. Jesus didn't react negatively to the suffering He experienced, because He trusted Himself to Him Who judges righteously. What an example for us when people are coming against us! If we can be quick to say, "I trust myself to Him Who judges righteously", it will release the power of Holy Spirit within us to carry us through victoriously! The reward comes when you are doing what God told you to do and you are ridiculed and insulted. Great is your reward in heaven! Rejoice!

> *Jesus went about all Galilee, preaching the gospel of the kingdom, and healing all kinds of sickness and all kinds of disease among the people.* (Matthew 4:23)

He preached and demonstrated the good news of the kingdom. He said,

> *"I must preach the kingdom of God to the other cities also, because for this purpose I have been sent."* (Luke 4:43)

That was His purpose and it should be ours as well. He came to demonstrate what it can be like to live on this earth, tapping into Father God for His wisdom and direction, His life and His purpose, His sustenance and His power, and His intimate Father-Son relationship. A kingdom is where there is a king ruling in power and authority.

Those things birthed in the flesh will not produce life, but only that which is birthed of the Spirit realm will produce life!

Jesus told us how to pray,

> *"Your kingdom come, Your will be done, on earth as it is in heaven."* (Matthew 6:10)

How will we know how to pray if we don't access heaven to see what is on the Father's heart? We must see what He is doing and hear what He is saying. Then we pray, "Let it be on earth as it is in heaven. Let's personalize this. "Your kingdom come in Me, through me, and all around me, as it is in heaven!" He went on to say,

> *"Seek first the kingdom of God and His righteousness, and all these things shall be added to you."* (Matthew 6:33)

He had been expressing that we need things and the Father knows it all. Seeking His kingdom first and determining His will, purpose, and glory will produce the miraculous. If you get filled with His Word and spend time listening to His spirit. It'll increase your faith and you'll create an atmosphere for understanding His will and His way. He told His disciples that it has been given to them to know the mysteries of the kingdom of heaven. (Matthew 13:11, Mark 4:11, Luke 8:10) He wants each of us, as well, to know the mysteries of the kingdom.

Jesus sent His disciples out to preach the kingdom of God and to heal the sick. They go hand in hand. We are not only to preach, but to demonstrate the kingdom of God. Demonstrate that He is the King and He is here with us! He heals and sets free today!

"How could I ever be qualified for this awesome life?" you have probably asked yourself. The awesome news is that you have already been qualified for it!

> *"The Father has qualified us to be partakers of the inheritance of the saints in the light. He has delivered us from the power of darkness and conveyed us into the kingdom of the Son of His love."* (Colossians 1:12,13)

The work has already been done! We just need to receive it and start walking in it! No matter what you have done in the past, you have been forgiven and qualified to take part in the inheritance! I have already been transferred out of the power of darkness! It has no power over me! I have been transferred into the kingdom of Jesus! I am in the kingdom! The kingdom of God is within me! The day I responded to God and asked Jesus into my life as Lord of my life, I received a heavenly transfer! Jesus is in me and I am in Jesus! I stepped out of myself and all my earthly limitations and I stepped into Jesus and all of His heavenly provision and ability! I began to move with Him in His power and ability!

How can this be?

For if by one man's offense (Adam's) death reigned through the one, much more those who receive abundance of grace and of the gift of righteousness will reign in life through the One, Jesus Christ. (Romans 5:17)

Grace is undeserved favor. Not one of us deserved it, but it has been provided for all of us who will receive it. The abundance of grace is much greater than our sin! The definition of abundance in this verse means surplus and superabundance. Wow! There is no sin too evil to be washed away by His grace! It's a free gift just for the receiving. Righteousness is a free gift also. Jesus became sin for us that we would become the righteousness of God in Christ Jesus. It's a free blessing and reward of being in Jesus! The promise here to those who will receive that abundance of grace is not that we will reign only when we get to heaven! It says we'll reign in life! Reign means to exercise kingly power, to govern, to exercise the highest influence. We are to receive an abundance of grace by faith and reign as the King's ambassadors! This promise is bringing life to my spirit even as I type. So many of us think we have disqualified ourselves from our destiny because of what we have done. We have allowed the devil to convince us that we are disqualified. If God has qualified us, who are we to disqualify ourselves? Now is the time to receive His superabundance of grace and His righteousness and reign in this life as we are called to do! We are to reign over the principalities and powers over our regions! We are to receive our instructions from the Heavenly Headquarters and move together as one body to reign!

When we receive a superabundance of grace, we will have an overflow to spill over into a lost and dying world and to

Christians who feel disqualified from the kingdom and from their callings. Receive that grace and allow it to flow! Let those people around you experience that grace through you so they will know that its a free gift and its theirs just for receiving it!

Jesus said, "The kingdom of God is within you!" (Luke 17:11)

What a treasure we have within us! God has placed His kingdom within us so that we can legislate over the earth. As we continually get God's perspective on what is going on in the earth, receive His battle plans and implement them on the earth, we will see the earth transformed all around us! How can we do this? Through exercising our voices in agreement with what God is saying through the power of the Holy Spirit. Our voices are powerful! I desire that He expand His kingdom in me and through me to the greatest degree possible! Your kingdom come, Lord! Your will be done on earth as it is in heaven!

God says,

"Behold, I will make you into a new threshing sledge with sharp teeth; You shall thresh the mountains and beat them small, and make the hills like chaff." (Isaiah 41:15)

Thresh means trample or strike repeatedly; separate wheat from the chaff.

In the above passage of scripture, God is saying He will make us into a threshing sledge. How can that be?

You have made him to have dominion over the works of Your hands; You have put all things under his feet. (Psalm 8:6)

The "him" He is talking about is man, male and female. We were created for dominion over all the earth. It's our purpose. I received a little chorus a few years back:

> *Come dance with Me*
> *Come dance with Me*
> *And you'll dance on the head of the enemy*
> *Come dance with Me*
> *Come dance with Me.*
> *And you'll dance on the head of the enemy.*
> *You'll dance on the head of the enemy.*

One form of threshing would be dancing on the head of the enemy. Another would be stamping. Another would be punching. The effective one would be whichever one God is showing you to do.

A *sledge* reminds me of the word sledgehammer that you pound something with in order to smash it.

Sharp teeth tells me that we will be using our mouths to destroy evil and to proclaim life and God's purpose into people and places. Mountains of opposition that have stood in our way for a very long time will be crumbled through our voices, as we allow the Holy Spirit to declare through us. We are called and equipped to radically change the course of history!

> *You shall winnow them, the wind shall carry them away, and the whirlwind shall scatter them; You shall rejoice in the Lord, and glory in the Holy One of Israel.* (Isaiah 41:16)

Winnow means remove by a current of air, get rid of something undesirable or unwanted, separating what is true and significant. The Holy Spirit moving through you will remove them!

We are called to rejoice and glory in the Holy One of Israel! Then God promises to do His part.

> *I will open rivers in desolate heights, and fountains in the midst of valleys, I will make the wilderness a pool of water, and the dry land springs of water. I will plant in the wilderness the ceder and the acacia tree, the myrtle and the oil tree; I will set in the desert the cypress tree and the pine and the box tree together, that they may see and know, and consider and understand together, that the hand of the Lord has done this, and the Holy One of Israel has created it.* (Isaiah 41:18-20)

He will send His river of life, His living water, and bring extreme fruitfulness! Let's rise up and do our part, which is threshing and winnowing! God will be faithful to do His part in opening rivers, fountains, pools, and springs, and flooding those places with His life! He will plant in the wilderness and the desert and bring fruitfulness, so people may see and know that the Lord has done it! This is how we take dominion as we were called to do. We have the privilege of working with God in bringing nations into alignment with His plan and purpose!

CHAPTER TEN

AXING THE ROOTS

How strong would a house be if it was not built on a strong foundation? We know that a house built on sand will not stand in the difficult storms of life. A house built on the Rock will stand through any storm. Jesus said,

> *"Therefore, whoever hears these sayings of Mine, and does them, I will liken him to a wise man who built his house on the rock."* (Matthew 7:24)

I keep picturing, in my mind, before a house is started and before the cement is poured, re-bar (steel rods with ridges) driven into the ground to support and strengthen the cement that is to be poured. What if that re-bar were made of rubber or even straw? Would it hold strong your foundation or your house? If you keep trying to build on the same foundation and every time a storm comes into your life you fall apart, it's time to look at the foundation or even the re-bar. I started out with a really messed up foundation. I had no self-worth, no direction, and felt of no value. When I personally experienced Jesus, Who is The Foundation for my new house, this adult person was ready to fly, but the little girl deep within was still a mess and needed some healing.

A vitally important part of preparation for ministry is taking the ax to the root. John the Baptist told the Pharisees and the Sadducees to:

> *"Bear fruits worthy of repentance. And even now the ax is laid to the root of the trees. Therefore every tree which does not bear good fruit is cut down and thrown into the fire."* (Matthew 3:8-10)

Not everything that has been planted in us is from God. In fact, most of it has been planted by someone else, either a family member, a teacher, a friend, yourself or the devil. It continues to grow in us just as the wonderful things planted by the Lord. Unless exposed and dealt with, it becomes rooted deeply within our heart. That's why it's necessary for us to take the ax to the root. It normally takes a negative incident to happen in order for it to be exposed. How does that happen? When a negative incident happens, we'll react very unreasonably and then wonder, "Where did that come from?" The answer is, "It came from deep within your heart."

> *The heart is deceitful above all things, and desperately wicked; Who can know it?* (Jeremiah 17:9)

Man has become very good at masking things. Many even hide behind the mask of ministry. We can smile and say everything is wonderful while our hearts are breaking. We can say we're people of faith while deep fears lurk within us. God loves us too much to allow anything that robs us of the intimate relationship He has designed and desires for us. He tries gently nudging us or speaking gently to us, but since we have deceived ourselves, the nudges seem to go right over our heads. What's a loving God to do? He allows something painful to happen to penetrate the veil we have covered our hearts with. At those times we become a little more open to question the cause. Usually we look around us and blame others and try everything else first. When we get no relief from the pain, we then may be open enough for Him to show us what the real root is and what is really deep within.

Are you brave enough to ask Him to show you the root cause? It is certainly to our advantage to do it. It's time for ungodly roots to be exposed. Normally the problem began with a painful experience. You nurtured a hurt. I'm not saying your pain wasn't valid. I'm sure that it was very valid. That's why you need Jesus to come heal that area. He's waiting for the invitation. Picture that situation where you were injured. Invite Jesus to come to that "you" that was injured. It could be the little toddler, a young child, an older child, a teenager, or an adult. Allow Him to come heal. Picture Him coming and watch and see what He does or says. Renounce your agreement with any spirit of darkness or death which entered your life at that time. It could be things like, "You're dirty." "You're stupid." "You're ugly." "You're not important." As you agreed with those thoughts and words, you gave him legal entry and empowered the enemy in that area of your life. You see, the devil wants to keep you from your destiny. He has strategies to defeat you and cause you not to press in to receive the blessings God has planned for you.

Pronounce that the contract is broken between you and the devil who has been feeding you the lies. Speak restoration over yourself in all those areas. Speak the opposite of what the devil has told you for many years. Be liberated to jump up into the arms of the Father and allow Him to give you the love you never received at that painful time. Allow Him to restore everything that was stolen or lost at that time, such as your innocence, your purity, your identity, your self-worth, your confidence, your mind and emotions, your joy, and your peace. God is not limited by time.

"Jesus Christ is the same, yesterday, today, and forever."
(Hebrews 13:8)

He knows the pain you felt and He is compassionate toward you. He promises to be near to the brokenhearted. His healing power can penetrate time and heal and restore emotionally, mentally, and physically.

Hurting people hurt people. We who desire to be in the ministry, which, in some capacity, should be all of us, must be set free from the effects of our hurts or we become a part of the vicious cycle that goes on and on from generation to generation. We all need restoration. Many shy away from this because they think it's too painful. They'll never be completely restored. It's sort of like restoring a house. You have to expose a major mess before you can start fixing, painting, and decorating it. Some never restore because they don't want to expose the mess necessary to bring restoration.

Many ungodly roots were inherited from your ancestors. You may have a tendency toward an ungodly activity that you have battled all of your life. You may have been asking yourself, "Where does that come from?" The sins of the fathers come down to the third and fourth generation. That doesn't seem fair. However the love of God comes down to a thousand generations. So, it is very rewarding to subject yourself to the cleansing process, in order to spare your children and their children. Then you can pass down to them the blessings and the love. Jesus redeemed us from the curse. Does that mean it is automatically done and we don't have to do anything?

Jesus said, "You shall know the truth and the truth shall set you free!" (John 8:32)

Invite the Holy Spirit to shine His light in you and show you the truth about you. He will be faithful to answer you and show you hidden areas, where there is anger, resentment, shame, guilt, condemnation, or fear. If it is generational, that which came through the bloodline can be renounced and broken in the name of Jesus by the blood of Jesus. If it came through something that happened to you or by your own activity, the above process will bring healing and restoration.

My husband and I missed our plane recently when we were traveling so I could speak at a conference. It cost a lot of money to get new tickets from another airline in order to arrive at the meeting on time. As we had to wait several hours for the next plane, I looked around and asked, "Okay, God, where's my divine appointment?" He highlighted a lady, who was knitting, sitting across from me. I struck up a conversation with her, and learned she was a Christian, who was also a Bible teacher. She mentioned she was battling anxiety and depression. I asked her if she knew what the root was. She told of a recent experience. I felt it went back farther than that but asked her to visualize herself in that situation and then visualize Jesus coming to the woman who looked like her. She did that and received much healing and release.

At that point Jerry wanted to go to lunch, so I excused myself. When we returned, we sat in different seats, farther away from the lady, as the previous seats were taken. The lady quickly jumped up, came and sat beside me, and leaned over and spoke into my ear. Weeping, she said, "That wasn't the real root. It was something that happened when I was ten years old." I encouraged her to see herself as that little girl and invite Jesus to come to her. She received a tremendous life-changing transformation, right there in the airport! She sent me a card later, declaring, "No more anxiety! No more depression!" She believed I had missed the plane for her benefit.

CHAPTER ELEVEN

DEVELOPING LISTENING SKILLS

Conversation adds life in a house. Without it, it becomes like a morgue. What if the conversation of your house was all one-sided? That would be called a monologue. If only one talked and never listened, not only would that one be boring to be around, but he wouldn't be very wise either, because he wouldn't have learned from others. He certainly would not be sensitive to the needs of others!

One thing that has stood out to me in my years of being active in the Christian church, as well as just living in the world, is the lack of listening skills. Have you ever gone to someone when you were really hurting and you just needed to talk out the problem and then receive some revelation and some healing? Immediately the other person began talking over you and believed he or she had the answer before really hearing the question. Often their answer had little to do with the actual question. There is such a need in the body of Christ to hear before speaking.

I already talked about the importance of hearing God speak and receiving initiatives from heaven before we come up with the answer. We ought also to hear each other before we begin to give the answer. How can you answer a question you haven't heard?

This has been a common problem and I've heard this complaint from many people: "I went to someone for help and I got a sermon before I got to tell him what I needed to say."

We have been given two ears and one mouth for a very good reason. We need to hear twice as much as we need to speak.

I remember when I was first saved at the age of twenty eight. Suddenly the truth of the sexual abuse I had suffered as a child was a huge reality and I needed some healing. It had been suppressed in me for many years. When I began to speak about it to someone in the church who I thought I could trust, I was quickly shut down with, "Don't talk about the past! It was all covered under the blood!" In my ignorance, I thought, "What the heck does that mean? I'm still hurting like crazy!" It was a while before I spoke to anyone about it again. (I forgave her long ago. She just had no understanding as she was raised in a good Christian home and had no idea how to minister to me.)

It's true that all of our sin was covered under the blood of Jesus and we are forgiven and cleansed by the blood. However, my soul is being restored as the Holy Spirit begins to uncover those things hidden by shame, I receive the revelation of how Satan used those things to trap me in silence, and I am empowered to forgive and release the injustices. Then it has no power over me! Until that time, I have anger and resentment, retaliation, rejection issues, feelings of being violated and entrapped, helplessness and hopelessness, mistrust, lust and impurity, and big-time control issues. Jesus said, "You shall know the truth and the truth shall set you free!" The truth doesn't set you free until you know it.

We, as ministers of the gospel, must listen, and ask the right questions led by the Holy Spirit. Then, as we listen to the Holy Spirit for the answers, we can help them to be set free!

Have you ever had someone finish your sentence in the way they thought you were going, and it was totally different than what you wanted to say? It would be really rare if you had not.

It boils down to the issue of honor and respect. When Jesus ministered to people, He always showed them respect, whether it was the woman caught in adultery or the one who had many husbands and was living with a man she had not married, or the woman with the issue of blood. He was always respectful to those to whom He wanted to minister and set free. We have much to learn from Him and His ways. When we talk right over someone, we are saying we have something much more important to say than they do. The root of that is pride. When we cut someone off in their conversation, it has the same root. It's pride. Pride is the only disease that makes everyone sick but the one who has it. We're to have the ministry of healing.

If someone continues going on and on about their problems, that's a different story. I'm not talking about that. Lovingly and respectfully, they need to be redirected in conversation and encouraged to begin speaking the answers.

I'm always amazed when I encounter young people in their twenties and ask them, "What's your dream?" Most of the time, they answer, "No one has ever asked me that before!" They have to stop and think about how to answer. Has no one taken enough interest in what they are feeling and desiring to ask them what is important to them and where they see themselves going? It's a perfect opportunity to then share with them that God wants to do, in and through their lives, above and beyond all they can ask or think or dream! It opens their hearts so they are ready to receive this Person Jesus, Who is so interested in them!

I was on an airplane returning from The Call, a large prayer gathering in Nashville led by Lou Engle. I was tired and ready for a nice rest on the plane. There was a young man wearing a red life bracelet sitting by the window. A young lady was sitting in the middle seat, and I had the aisle seat. I assumed the couple was traveling together and that they also were returning from The Call. I thought to myself, "Ah, no one needs Jesus here, so I can rest." I closed my eyes. I felt stirred in my spirit, and sat up. I asked the young lady next to me, "Are you returning from The Call?" She answered, "What's The Call?" I thought, "Oops, wrong judgment there!" I asked, "Are you not with this young man?' She said, "No." I then explained to her about the prayer gathering. "Sounds interesting," she commented. I then asked her about herself. She was on an educational trip.

"What's your dream?" I asked her. "Financial business," she answered.

I went on to say, "You know, it's good to get education and I'm sure God is in it in order to bring you to your destiny. He has given you a dream and if you add God to the mix, He'll take you farther than you can ever get on your own."

I explained my story of not being raised Christian, of my encounter with Jesus, and the amazing things God has done in my life since! I then asked, "Would you like to ask Jesus to come into your heart and take over your life?"

Immediately she answered, "Yes, I would!" I then prayed with her and led her to Jesus.

"Have you ever read the Bible?" I asked her.
"No"
"Do you have a Bible?"
"No"
"Would you like to have one?"
"Yes"

I gave her my new travel Bible that I had just purchased. She was thrilled! I showed her the book of Mark and suggested she start there. She immediately began reading it and read for some time!

I then told her some about the Holy Spirit. "Would you like me to pray for you to be filled with the Holy Spirit?"

"Yes!"

I did. She was twenty years old. Her parents came from India. I asked her if she traveled to India frequently. She said, "Yes." I told her that God would use her to tell family and friends there about Jesus. She received that.

In another incident, as one evening we traveled across the lake, on a twenty-two minute boat ride to the Chemehuevi Indian Reservation, where we pastored the church, I had just sat down in the boat and a young man came and sat beside me. I asked him, "What's your dream?" His answer was, "To be a rapper." I asked him, "Do you write rap songs?" He said, "Yes". He reached into his pocket and drew out a piece of paper. On it were the words to his latest one. It was obvious from the words that he was searching for light. I shared with him that He could know personally the one who is the the Light, Who would inspire him to write life-giving songs that would impact his generation. Before we reached the other side of the lake, he had asked Jesus into his heart and invited Him to inspire his songs. I asked him if he had a Bible. He did not, but he wanted one. I told him I would get him one. Before I could get it to him, a couple of days later, he had walked to the church and asked for his Bible!

There are so many young people hungry for someone to care about them. Everyone needs to know they are valued and significant. We, as believers, claim to know personally the One Who sees us as valued and significant. That revelation changed my life! Should not we be the ones who carry that revelation within us, and release it to all we meet? Not with an "I know something you don't know" attitude, or an "I'm better than you are" attitude, but, with humility and respect, we should see each one as significant and treat them accordingly. There is something we can learn from each person we meet. God wants to release His life and His love to each one, as well. Look with the eyes of God! Listen with your heart to what is on their hearts. See what God sees! Hear what He is saying! Then release it to each individual and see life and light enter in, right in front of your eyes!

CHAPTER TWELVE

BATHING IN GOD'S LOVE

How complete and effective would your house be without a bathtub or a shower? Just as I need to take a bath or shower daily, I need a daily love bath, soaking in the love of God. One of my very favorite soaking verses is this:

> *See what an incredible quality of love the Father has given (shown, bestowed on) us that we should be permitted to be named and called and counted the children of God! And so we are!* (1 John 3:1a Amplified Bible)

Another version talks of the love the Father lavished on us. Pause and meditate on that. See yourself flooded with the love of the Father. Allow that love to saturate every part of your being. This is perhaps the most important chapter in this book, because, without love, we are nothing. According to 1 Corinthians 13:2, you can be a great prophet, or a great faith minister who can cast mountains into the sea, or have great knowledge and spiritual understanding of mysteries, and yet, if you don't have love, you are nothing.

I have found that I need frequent love baths. How do I take a love bath? This is what works for me every time. I meditate on 1 John 4;7-18. I don't just read over it, I chew on it as a cow chews its cud.

> *Beloved, let us love one another, for love is of God; and everyone who loves is born of God and knows God. He who does not love does not know God, for God is love.* (1 John 4:7,8)

There's no other way to interpret this. If you're not loving, you're not even born again and you don't know God. That eliminates my nasty attitude in a big hurry! To know anyone, you must spend time in their presence, listening to them. So in God's presence, His love is emanated toward us, because that's Who He is: Love personified.

> *In this the love of God was manifested toward us, that God has sent His only begotten Son into the world, that we might live through Him. In this is love, not that we loved God, but that He loved us and sent His Son to be the propitiation for our sins.* (1 John 4:9,10)

A picture's worth a thousand words. I keep hearing those words. Here's the clearest picture of God's love we'll ever get. Our loving Father sent the best that He had, His only Son, into a place filled with darkness and death, to convey to us His great love. He sent Him to take upon Himself all of our sin, so that it could be nailed to the cross. Now as painful as that would be to have nails pounded into my hands and feet, it would be unbearably more painful to become the combined sin of the whole world. Think about your worst sin and the burden and weight of heaviness it was upon you. Think of all of just your sin and the weight that would be. Now multiply it millions of times. To think of it is unbearable! He actually became it and carried it so that it could be nailed to the cross and put to death once and for all! Why did He do that? God was manifesting His love toward you and me so we could live through Him. To get the full benefit, you must picture yourself on the cross, because He was representing you that day. Picture that old you dead and buried in the tomb. Now picture Jesus in you, instead of the old you, being raised from the dead, filled with resurrection power and ascending into Heaven. There's the victory. Now you can live in resurrection power, free from the power of sin and death. You can live through Him! See yourself going into Him. Now, saturated with Him, live your life through Him!

The big deal is not that we love God. The big deal is that He loved us and sent His Son to be the payment for our sins. That's some kind of love!

Beloved, if God so loved us, we also ought to love one another. No one has seen God at any time. If we love one another, God abides in us, and His love has been perfected in us. (1 John 4:11,12)

God places people in our lives that are difficult to love in our own flesh. The purpose for that is so we have to spend time bathing in the love of God until His love floods us and can flow through us to those people. That's how His love is perfected in us. Perfected here means "brought to maturity, completed, accomplished, fulfilled. That's how the fruit of the Spirit is worked into us. When Jesus told us to be perfect, He was saying, "Be openhearted." That's the literal translation for perfect in that verse.

Our Father is so openhearted toward us. Even while we were steeped in sin and rebellion, He opened His heart toward us & sent His Son to die in our place.

> *God demonstrates His own love toward us in that while we were still sinners, Christ died for us.* (Romans 5:8)

That is mind blowing to me! I remember well what I was like before Jesus showed Himself to me. I certainly didn't deserve His love. I'm so glad His love for me doesn't depend on my righteousness, but only His.

His love is always perfect and His love dwells in me. We need to bathe in that truth for a while. I don't get to choose who to love and who not to love, because God's love is no respecter of persons. It is unconditional.

When His love is expressed through us, we know that we abide in Him and He in us. His Spirit dwells in us, and it's the Spirit of love.

> *Whoever confesses that Jesus is the son of God, God abides in him, and he in God. And we have known and believed the love that god has for us. God is love, and he who abides in love abides in God, and God in him.* (1 John 4:15,16)

Not only does God abide (dwell, live continually, vitally united to, remain fixed, continues) in us, but we live in Him. Pause and think of that. Step out of yourself and step into God. Become a part of Him and what He is doing.

It's His desire that we know personally, experientially the love of God. We must believe the love God has for us and receive it personally. God is love, so if we are living in that love, we're living in God and He's living in us.

> *Love has been perfected among us in this, that we may have boldness in the day of judgment, because as He is, so are we in this world.* (1 John 4:17)

We'll have no holy boldness in this life if we are not living in that love. That verse doesn't say that when we get to heaven we'll have His love perfected in us. It reads, "As He is, so are we in this world." We are to be the representation of the Father's love in this world, not just to the nice people, but to the wicked sinner. How else will they know the Father's love is real? His love will not only give us boldness in this life, but in the day of judgment.

> *There is no fear in love, but perfect love casts out fear, because fear involves torment. But he who fears has not been made perfect in love.* (1 John 4:18)

Most of us are walking around in some kind of fear. The devil is always coming at us with something to fear, because it robs us of faith. He is very afraid of people walking in faith. Everyone's area of vulnerability to fear is a little different, but nonetheless, we all have some area of vulnerability to fear that Satan can torment us with.. The above scriptures are my remedy to removing fear. The word fear in this verse is phobos, from which we get the English word phobia, which means, "that which causes flight."

I grew up in a lot of fear, so that was an area of vulnerability I had to deal with, and , on occasion, it still tries to slip in. That's when I run to these scriptures, which bring me back into the love of God. I soak in His love, and fear leaves. It's not possible to be soaking in the love of God and feel fearful, because there is no fear in love. It sounds almost too simple, but it's true. God's truth is pretty simple.

We love Him because He first loved us. (1 John 4:19)

If we don't get that revelation of God's awesome unconditional love for us, we will be incapable of loving Him, or anyone else.

A great example of His love is found in Hosea, who was a righteous prophet that God used to demonstrate His love for His people that are always whoring after other loves. He told Hosea to go marry a prostitute, which Hosea obediently did. He showed her love over and over; yet she continued in her old lifestyle. She had a son, then a daughter and another son. The last was named Lo-Ammi, meaning "Not My People", which meant it wasn't even his baby. She ran off to her lovers, thinking they could supply her needs better than Hosea and she stayed until she was no longer beneficial to her lovers and was being sold in the marketplace.

> *Then the Lord said to Hosea, "Go again, love a woman who is loved by a lover and is committing adultery, just like the love of the Lord for the children of Israel, who look to other gods and love the raisin cakes of the pagans. So I bought her for myself for fifteen shekels of silver, and one and one-half homers of barley.* (Hosea 3:1, 2)

That was about four tenths of an ounce of silver and five bushels of barley. She wasn't worth too much money at that point in her life. Hosea was obedient to the voice of the Lord. What a price Hosea had to pay to fulfill His calling. He was called to be a prophetic picture of God's love to us.

So many people have become disillusioned with the church and have returned to other loves, primarily due to offenses or perceived offenses or because they feel they are being deprived in some way. They are back out in the world running after other loves. We must pray for them and refrain from judgment and be ready to welcome them back into the fold and love them. It would be wonderful if it were only those outside the church that are running after other loves, but many in the church, even some leaders, are also running after other things We often do what is comfortable or popular, rather than step out in faith and do as God is saying. We, as leaders, must guard against becoming people-pleasers and watering down messages. We are called to please God first. It is His church. If we're not careful, we can just do the religious stuff and do what's always worked in the past. God is a creative God and is full of creativity. He wants to express Himself in new and fresh ways to His people. As we soak in His love, He will speak to us creative ideas of how to express His love to people. He abounds in love and faithfulness. He keeps His covenant of love. His love reaches to the heavens. His faithfulness reaches to the clouds. He loves you with an everlasting love and His banner over you is love.

CHAPTER THIRTEEN

VISITING CAMP COMPARISON

How satisfied will you be with your new house if you are constantly comparing it to a newer or bigger or better home? I love looking at model homes to see what the latest and greatest design or decor is, or what the newest appliances or gadgets are. However, it can be dangerous for me because it causes an avarice spirit to rise up in me. I start imagining what my house should look like, and soon I am discontent or even disgruntled with what I have. The following allegory is based upon a true experience I had, out of which evolved, for me, an important life teaching.

I took a trip one day a number of years ago and ended up in a faraway land, where confusion and darkness and despair dwell. I didn't intend to travel that far. In fact, I didn't plan the trip at all. I was too tired to travel to begin with, but it happened so quickly that I surprised myself when I ended up where I did.

It began with a little thought...a comparative thought, like, "This is not going the way I had planned." That's where the trip should have ended. I should have heeded the warning. "Stop! The door's open!" I didn't hear the warning. I just sauntered through the door. I had entered Camp Comparison.

Comparison was there to greet me at the gate and made me feel most welcome. He made many suggestions, which I foolishly heeded, and I began to compare what was happening with what I thought should have happened. From there it went to comparing the ministry with others around it. From there I began to compare the success of my personal ministry with those around me. Then I began to compare "me" with others around me. Comparison said, "Look at Dennis and Lynnie. They're traveling the world and starting ministries. You were told thirty-four years ago in prophecies that you would be an establisher for the Kingdom of God all over the world. What happened to you? Who do you think you are pastoring a church anyway?"

Other campers soon arrived to join us. Discouragement presented himself and I fellowshipped with him awhile. In fact, we decided to sit a spell on a log. He had lots to say, like "You know, it never goes the way you hope. All of your prayer and hard work really doesn't get you anywhere."

Another new friend dressed in green appeared. His name was Envy. He brought with him a cloud of darkness I had not experienced for some time. He made me desire and even covet what others had in their ministries. I felt life being sucked out of me. Fear and Confusion then came hand in hand and sat in on this fellowship of Non- Believers. My thinking seemed foggy and I began to lose focus. I was trying to function in a normal fashion but found it very difficult.

Suddenly Depression, a guy all suited up in gray, loomed overhead, riding on a massive dark cloud that so seemed to fill the atmosphere with darkness, that, when he swooped down, all I could see was him and his big ugly friends, Doom and Gloom.

Failure soon came out of the woods and sat on a log beside us. He imparted some of his great worldly wisdom like, "You really blew this one! You seem to fail at everything you do. If you had only done things differently, you wouldn't have failed so badly." The "you should haves" and "If you had onlys" and "You could haves", and "If you hadn'ts" flowed from his mouth like vomit, until I heard, "You're a failure!"

Off in the distance I saw Despair coming my way. I could hardly see him for the black clouds that enveloped him. Suddenly I began to realize I was in deep trouble and I fell into bed exhausted.

After a very restless night, I awoke the next morning and ran to my Father God. I said, "God, we have to talk! Something's very wrong! I feel so confused. I don't know what you want. I'm disappointed and angry. It never seems to go the way I think it's going to. Ouch! Is that the problem, Lord? I'm making plans for You? God, help me! I repent of my attitude."

Light began to come in and I continued. "I repent of the sin of comparing. I repent of envy. It's ugly. It sucks the life out of me. I'm sorry for the mentality I've passed on to others, that things have to happen in a certain way. That's pride. It's not up to me to decide how it's going to go or how things are going to happen. I'm sorry God, for falling short of Your glory."

Then I began to hear God. He then assured me that the night I was so concerned about had gone just as He had planned and it was strategic in His plan. Sometimes He allows things to go totally different than what I planned in order to expose me and my attitude, my sin, or someone else's. It may not even be about me!

I had spent a day fellowshipping with a comparing spirit. It had brought darkness, heaviness, irritability, judgment of self and ministry, confusion, anger, fear, envy, depression, and despair. I had opened the door and invited all of these in.

The Lord impressed me, "I have told you from the beginning that your assignment will be different. If you compare with those around you, you will always come up short. Throw away the measuring stick. Line yourself up with Me and My plan for you and only you! It will free you to see Me more clearly, to see your purpose more clearly, and to enjoy life along the way much more!"

For we dare not class ourselves or compare ourselves with those who commend themselves. But they, measuring themselves by themselves, and comparing themselves among themselves, are not wise. (II Corinthians 10:12)

CHAPTER FOURTEEN

DON'T BITE THE BAIT

Do you have a tall fence around your house to keep away anyone who might try to hurt you? That same fence is probably keeping out others who could be a blessing to you. Perhaps it's a neighbor who would want to bless your household with a plate of delicious warm cookies, but because of the tall fence, she doesn't feel welcome. There have been times I have been deeply hurt by someone and I've been tempted to cut them out of my life. God has been quick to whisper, "No, don't do it. I'm going to use her in your life and I'm going to use you in her life, for I have plans for you together." Amazingly, that has taken place repeatedly.

A while back some friends and I were praying and seeking God's heart for our city. One man saw a fence, with people enclosed in it. He asked God, "What's the fence?" Instantly I heard, "The fence is offense." Knowingly or unknowingly, we, the church, have offended many people and that is why they have closed themselves off to the church. I felt the grieving of Father's heart for His people who have been hurt. Many times the church has spoken truth, but it was accompanied with arrogance and pride. At that time, I felt an unction to pray and ask God, on behalf of the church, to forgive us for all the offenses we have caused. We asked God to please release all those enclosed by the fence of offense and show us how to reconcile them to God and to the church.

The number one attack of the enemy is to get you to be offended. He's not really particular who you are offended at, as long as you are offended, although he prefers it is someone in the church, so he can get you to abandon fellowship. If he can get you isolated from other believers, it's much easier to take you down and destroy your testimony, and ultimately your life and your destiny.

Satan sets a trap to see if he can get you to fall into it. The word offense, in the Greek, literally means, "the name of the part of the trap to which the bait is attached, the trap or snare itself. It normally arouses prejudice, or becomes a hindrance to others, or causes them to fall by the way."

We must guard our hearts by making a choice not to be offended, no matter what. When an offense comes, it helps if you immediately declare, "I choose not to be offended!" Does that mean it doesn't hurt? No. Even though it hurts, continue to declare it. The hurt will dissipate much sooner, and you will see the rewards of your effort.

The following is an example of how that works. One day I ran into a friend of our family, who immediately, to my surprise, started to harshly criticize me and my family. His most stinging words were, "and you call yourself a Christian!" I walked away in shock as he had never said a negative word to me, prior to that time, and I had felt we had a good relationship. I felt pain in my heart, but realized that it was absolutely necessary for me to make the choice not to be offended. I began to declare, "I choose not to be offended! I forgive him." I continued to hurt for a few days. I heard in my spirit and spoke with my mouth, "Behold the Lamb of God Who takes away the sins of the world." I began to focus on Jesus and declare, "The blood of the

Lamb is flowing down over him." I visualized him saturated with the blood of the Lamb. The hurt began to leave. I began to feel God's love for the man.

Within a few days, I was driving through the area where the man lived, as I was going to visit my friend Suzie. He was outside and saw me and came running out to the car. I stopped. He actually opened the car door and got into the passenger seat and began apologizing to me, saying, "I'm so sorry I said those things to you. I have no idea where those things came from. That's not how I feel at all. Will you forgive me?"

I responded, "Of course! I already have!" He got out of the car, and I just began praising God for His power and for the power in the blood! The blood will never lose its power! Holding onto an offense clogs up the flow of God in us. Allowing an offense to stay initiates all kinds of problems, emotionally, mentally, and physically, as well as spiritually. The one who has been offended has more power to pray for the offender than anyone else, because it's necessary to tap into the Spirit realm, in order to do it.

A number of years ago, I was working as a resort convention center coordinator. I had just finished preparing the center for a wedding and I thought the room looked beautiful. My supervisor entered the scene and criticized the way it was setup and told me to change it. I was irritated, but I did as she asked. I allowed the offense to grow and I continued thinking about it. "How dare she criticize my wonderful job! Who does she think she is? Why did she wait until I had it all done to come in and ax it?" I began to feel rejection, then anger, then hostility.

I was outside where part of the festivities were taking place. As I was walking down a hill, I twisted my foot and began to feel excruciating pain. I had to function in pain for the rest of the night. At the end of the event I went in to sit at my desk and elevate my foot, applying ice to it. One of the servers came in and saw I was in pain. She said, "Well, you've prayed for me and it worked. I'll pray for you." She laid hands on my foot and prayed. Nothing happened.

I went home that night, still in pain, applying ice on my foot. In fact, I couldn't sleep because of the pain. I kept saying, "Lord, you have to heal me! Tuesday I speak at Aglow on overcoming the enemy. This would be a lousy witness to Your power!" Nothing happened.

Finally, after battling this for a few hours, the Lord said, "You're angry at your sister. You're holding onto an offense." Immediately I responded by admitting my anger and repenting. I let go of the offense and spoke, "I forgive her in Jesus name!"

Then I prayed for my foot again. To my amazement, the pain immediately left and the swelling disappeared! I was totally healed!

I'm not making a doctrine out of this. Holding onto an offense is not always the cause of the pain or infirmity. However, it's always wise to check your heart and ask God to show you if there is an offense in there that could be obstructing God's Spirit from moving and His healing power from flowing through you.

If you are in pain at this time, I suggest you do this right now. Ask God to shine His light into your heart and expose any hindrance hidden in there. Then renounce it, forgive, release the offense, and let go of it.

Unforgiveness adds undue stress to your heart, your mind, your emotions, and your body. Getting rid of the offense releases the perfect law of liberty, which is love. You'll experience a greater freedom in many areas of your life!

CHAPTER FIFTEEN

DANCING UPON INJUSTICE

What would a house be like without a toilet to flush down "poop" or a garbage disposal to disintegrate the garbage? It would become a pretty messy and smelly house, don't you agree? Often we are holding onto things, in our personal house, that are messy and smelly as well. I liken this to holding on to the injustices you have suffered, those things that eat at you, which will eventually impact every area of your life.

God wants us to know that He is a God of justice.

The Lord is a God of justice. (Isaiah 30:18)

He's a God of truth and without injustice. (Deuteronomy 32:4)

All of His ways are justice. (Daniel 4:37)

I discovered a few years ago that there is a connection between how we react to injustice, and receiving the favor of God, as well as, having favor with man. Do you know that God wants you to walk in the divine favor?

Injustice, according to Webster's Dictionary, is absence of justice, violation of rights, unfairness, and an act that inflicts undeserved hurt. Who has not experienced an injustice? No one I know. An injustice, whether real or perceived, can have the same effect on a person.

I read in the Arizona Republic that, according to an FBI agent, "Serial killers aim to right some sense of injustice. Once they start, they lose their sense of right and wrong. They have a commonality that they've been wronged and want to unleash their rage." These serial killers are viewing life through the spirit of injustice.

I believe there is a spirit of injustice that causes that kind of reaction. When we continue to walk in injustice and the effects of injustice and have not dealt with it, that spirit attaches itself to us, and we begin to view life through that spirit of injustice.

A number of years ago, I read a verse of scripture that greatly impacted my life!

> *What injustice have your fathers found in Me, that they have gone far from Me, have followed idols, and have become idolaters?* (Jeremiah 2:4)

What has happened to all of the people who came into church, got excited about Jesus, and then, after a season, disappeared? I believe, if we could talk to them all, the greatest majority of them have felt they were treated with injustice.

When we have been treated unjustly, and we carry that injustice, we first pull away from people, and then we pull away from God, as we begin to think the injustice came from Him. Soon we have pulled back far from Him. We began to serve the spirit of injustice rather than serving God. That spirit becomes an idol. An idol can be an image, which we have carved in our minds, of God, of others, or of self.

Injustice will try to build a wall between you and your destiny. It's very possible that the ones you have walled yourself off from are the very ones God wants to use to help you achieve your destiny. We've built a fence of injustices, and have come to believe that it is safe behind the fence. Quite the opposite is true, because when the devil isolates, he can easily attack, conquer and devour people. That's his goal. It's easy for him to deceive you when you are separated because you stop listening to the truth and start believing the lies.

God has called each one of us to greatness. His plans for us are above and beyond what we could ever ask or think.

Have you ever had dreams of greatness?

Joseph was a young man of seventeen who dreamed of greatness. God had given him a dream and the dream had greatly impacted him! That dream sustained him through all his trials.

He shared that dream with his brothers, which was a big mistake. It's not a good idea to share dreams with those who are jealous of you or hate you. They will use it against you. People have two different reactions to someone's dreams, when they don't understand them. They either keep the matters in mind or they envy you.

The devil will always try to kill your dreams. God is always there to fulfill your dreams.

Joseph's brothers were feeding the flocks in Shechem. Their father sent Joseph to check on them. When the brothers saw him far off, they conspired to kill him. (Isn't it strange how your enemies think that if they can get rid of you, they'll be blessed?) They called Joseph "the dreamer", mocking him. Remember how Isaac was called the child of promise and Ishmael, his brother, mocked him? I believe there is a generational spirit of mocking that is always trying to hinder or stop the plans of God from coming forth.

Most of the brothers wanted to kill him. (That spirit of Cain) Rueben suggested they just throw him into a pit in the wilderness. He planned to rescue him later and bring him back home.

They stripped Joseph of his tunic, gave him no water or food, and cast him into a pit. Then they sat down to eat a meal. What kind of brother casts you into a pit, without food or water, and sits down and enjoys a meal? Talk about an injustice!

Then they looked up and saw some Midianite traders and it hit them that they could make some money on the deal by selling Joseph to them. So they sold him for twenty shekels of silver, the fair price for a male slave. His own brothers profited by selling him! More injustice! They lied about him and told his father that he was dead.

The Midianites sold Joseph to Potiphar, an officer of Pharaoh. Did Joseph cop an attitude during this time? Obviously not, because he received favor with Potiphar.

> *The Lord was with Joseph and he was a successful man; and he was in the house of his master the Egyptian.* (Genesis 39:2)

Keeping your heart right in difficult times will bring you favor. You can only do that in the power of the Lord. Joseph had a personal relationship with the Lord that kept his heart pure and brought him success.

> *And his master saw that the Lord was with him and that the Lord made all he did to prosper in his hand.* (Genesis 39:3)

The Lord was obviously with Joseph and he had favor! No matter where you go, you can take God's blessing if you stay in the right attitude. If you are quick to release the injustice and don't allow bitterness, even unbelievers will see the favor of God upon you!

> *So Joseph found favor in his sight, and he served him. Then he made him overseer of his house, and all that he had he put under his authority.* (Genesis 39:4)

Joseph had such favor that he was given authority over all Potiphar had! We see that there is a connection between releasing injustices and receiving favor and there's also a connection between receiving favor and receiving Godly authority.

Because the blessing of the Lord was upon Joseph, the Lord blessed Potiphar's house and the blessing of the Lord was on all he had in the house and in the field. The devil didn't like that, so he had to devise another plan. He inspired Potiphar's wife to try to seduce him. She tried over and over to get him to go to bed with her and Joseph wouldn't bite the bait. She finally got him alone in the house and grabbed him by his garment and tried again to get him in bed with her. He ran, leaving his garment with her. She was so angry at being rejected by Joseph that she lied about him. She said he had tried to seduce her and when she screamed, he fled, leaving his garment behind. Naturally Potiphar was angry at Joseph and threw him into prison.

Another injustice! Joseph could have whined, "I didn't do anything wrong, God. I was a faithful servant. Why did this awful thing happen to me, God? Why this injustice?"

Did Joseph cop an attitude? Obviously not!

> *But the Lord was with Joseph and showed him mercy, and He gave him favor in the sight of the keeper of the prison. And the keeper of the prison committed to Joseph's hand all the prisoners who were in the prison; whatever they did there, it was his doing. The keeper of the prison did not look into anything that was under Joseph's authority, because the Lord was with him, and whatever he did, the Lord made it prosper.* (Genesis 39: 21-23)

Even in prison, the Lord was with Joseph and showed him mercy and gave him great favor! Whatever he did, the Lord made it to prosper! He was given authority even in prison!

The king's butler and his baker offended the king and they were thrown into prison with Joseph. Each of them had a dream that they couldn't interpret. Joseph knew His God was able to interpret dreams, so he told them to tell him the dreams. God gave Joseph the interpretation of each dream. He said the baker would be hanged and the butler would be restored to the king. Joseph told the butler to remember him when he got out and to mention him to the king so he could get out of prison. When the butler got out of prison, he forgot all about Joseph.

What an injustice! Did Joseph hold on to that injustice? No!

Two years later Pharaoh had a dream. No one could interpret his dream. All of a sudden, the butler remembered Joseph and told the king about him. The king sent for Joseph and asked him to interpret his dream. Joseph interpreted the prophetic dream concerning Egypt, that there would be seven years of plenty and seven years of famine. He told him God would shortly bring it to pass; to put a wise man over Egypt and appoint officers and collect one fifth of the produce in the plentiful years and store up for the famine.

Look at Pharaoh's response!

"Can we find such a one as this, a man in whom is the Spirit of God? Inasmuch as God has shown you all this, there is no one as discerning and wise as you." (Genesis 41:38, 39)

Joseph was just thirty years old and the king was so impressed with his connection with God that he made him governor of the whole land! He had more authority than anyone, except the king! Even the heathens will be impressed when we allow the Spirit to move freely through us!

After the seven years of plenty in Egypt ended, the seven years of famine began as Joseph said. The famine was over all the earth, so people were coming, from all over, to Joseph to buy grain.

When Joseph's father Jacob saw that there was grain in Egypt, he sent his ten sons, all but Benjamin, down to buy grain. Joseph recognized his brothers but they didn't recognize him. Then Joseph remembered the dreams he had as a teenage boy. He played with his brothers a little bit and sent one of them back to get Benjamin, his youngest brother and put the rest in prison for three days to test them. They said to one another, "We are truly guilty concerning our brother. That's why this has happened to us. His blood is now required of us."

Joseph heard them. They didn't realize that he spoke their language because he spoke to them through an interpreter. When he heard them, he cried. He released them and they bowed down before him, just as he had seen in his dream. He finally told them he was Joseph.

Joseph didn't blame God. He didn't blame his brothers. He told them God had sent him before them to prepare the way for them, for their deliverance. He said, "It wasn't you who sent me here, but God." He saw the whole thing through God's perspective. He didn't give them justice. He gave them mercy.

We've been talking about injustice, major injustice and how God can turn it for our good if we stay in a right attitude. Injustice happens to us all. How we react to it is up to us.

When injustice happens to us and we don't deal with it in a godly manner, it attaches itself to us and eats at us like a parasite. It destroys us on the inside and seems to attract more and more injustice like a magnet, until we feel no one is for us anymore. It invites a spirit of injustice that, until taken authority over and cast out, beckons injustice to us. God wants us free, free to give love and to receive love. God loves justice. That's his plan for you. He's a God of truth and without injustice. Some of us are still stuck on the injustice. I know. I used to be there.

I grew up with an abusive dad. There was a lot of violence and verbal abuse. When I was around eleven, my father began sexually abusing me. At age seventeen a teacher stepped way over the line with me and pinned me against a wall. At eighteen I married a verbally abusive husband. When I went to a priest for help, he tried to seduce me. There was a pattern of repeated injustices. It seemed to be a way of life. I didn't realize that the seed of injustice had been planted in me and acted as a magnet, drawing injustice to me in all areas of life.

You can't receive the favor of God when you are bound up in injustice. God wants to break the chains of injustice from you and replace it with His favor, favor with God and favor with man.

When I finally answered the call to be a pastor in 1997, some didn't think I should be because I was a woman. That had been my argument for years. After breaking the chain of injustice, I now have such favor with pastors!

I had just received the revelation on injustice when I went to Paris, France to minister with Lynnie Walker. The first day in Paris was Lynnie's birthday and I said I would take her and the pastor to lunch. We were seated in a little cafe when the pastor began to talk about something that was really bothering her, that she just couldn't put a handle on. The word injustice came to my mind instantly. "It's injustice," I said. Immediately the pastor said, "That's it!" and she began to speak, "I release the injustice of..." filling in the blanks over and over again. Lynnie and I sat and watched her come into more and more freedom the more she released. She paused and Lynnie began to speak. The pastor exclaimed, "No! No!" She continued, "I'm not done! There's more!" She continued for what seemed like twenty minutes, releasing injustices all the way back to her youth! When she finally finished, she was glowing! "I feel so free!" she declared. She looked free, as her countenance had changed! She asked me to minister on injustice at her church.

The next evening we were in her apartment overlooking the Eiffel Tower. She had invited ladies to come to her home for a dinner meeting. She was busy preparing food and Lynnie was busy preparing the message she was going to give that night. The doorbell rang, and it was a young woman named Arlette. She staggered in and fell on the sofa. She had great difficulty walking or talking, because of a great physical handicap. The Lord said, "Ask her about injustices". When I did, she began to tell me, with great difficulty, about the many injustices she had experienced. I encouraged her to speak release to each injustice, one by one. Amazingly, as she did that she spoke more and more clearly. I asked her if she could lift her arms and praise the Lord. She said she was unable to lift her arms like that, but she did it. I asked her if she could sing. She replied, "I've always wanted to sing, but I can't." She began to sing. I asked her if she wanted to dance. She got up and danced around the room, singing with great joy! Later I found out she had Parkinson's disease, as well as other problems. God showed Himself so awesome that evening, as I saw the power of releasing injustices!

In 2006 we were being given a lease for land on the Chemehuevi Indian Reservation, where we were pastors. We were told we needed a survey. We had little money, so Bill at the tribal real estate office said he would talk to the surveyor they use and he was sure it would be fairly reasonable. We said, "Okay." We didn't receive a bill and it had been a month, so I stopped in to see Bill and asked him about the bill. He said, "We have it, but it's quite expensive. I'll see if I can get him to lower it." I stopped in a few times after that and got the same response. After two months, I finally said, "Just give me the bill." It was for $1040. I too was shocked at the amount.

I came home and called the surveyor and asked him if he could lower the bill any for the church. He was upset because it had been two months since he had done the job and had received no payment. He wouldn't listen when I tried to explain I had just received the bill. He got very angry and shouted, "If I had known it was for a church, I wouldn't have even done it! Just pay the bill now!"

I looked in the checkbook, and surprisingly, we had that amount in there. That was a real rarity. I wrote out the check and put it in an envelope addressed to the surveyor. I took it down to his office, which was closed for the rest of the day, so I put it in the mail at the post office. I said, "Lord, I lift this up to you. I believe this money is coming back to us and I'm not even going to have to ask for it and I thank you now for it in Jesus name!" I saw a picture in my mind of walking into the surveyor's office and a man handing me a check. I released the injustice and went on to pray for the salvation of that man and prayed blessings on him. I said, "Lord, he needs salvation more than we need the money. I just pray for him to be saved. Go after him, Lord." I began to thank God for that man's salvation.

A few months went by, and we didn't have enough money to pay the church bills. We were $1,000 short. I asked, "Lord, what do you want me to do?" Instantly I heard, "Go see the surveyor." I felt an excitement rise up in my spirit. I planned to go the next morning, and I began to pray that God would prepare his heart.

The next morning I picked up my granddaughter Alyssa and we went down to the surveyor's office. I walked in and asked to see him. The secretary asked, "Will he know what you want?" I hesitated and then spoke, "Yes, I believe so."

She went in to tell him and the man came right out and invited me into his office. He began apologizing all over the place. He said, "I don't know why I talked to you like that. I can't believe I talked to you like that." I just stood there smiling at him. He asked me, "So, is there any good thing happening over there on that reservation?" I answered, "Oh yes, people are getting saved and getting off alcohol and drugs. There are lots of good things happening over there." Then he told me he had been baptized a few weeks ago. He said, "I can't give you back your check because I have a partner and he wouldn't understand, but I'll tell you what I'm going to do. I'm going to write you a check from my own personal checking account." He got out his checkbook, wrote a check and handed me a check for $1,040 and I had never even mentioned the money!

One more testimony of God's favor took place in Brazil. I was ministering there at a women's conference with Lynnie Walker and Rita Krsief. We had an hour or two of free time to shop. I bought a couple of sweaters for about $12 each. Lynnie had picked one out also, so I just paid for all three of them. Lynnie had been given money to buy herself something real nice, so she then chose a little boutique to shop in. I looked at a few prices and quickly decided the prices were too steep for me, so I stood back and waited while Lynnie was trying on some clothes. Suddenly the store owner came out from behind the counter and handed me a beautiful bright pink blouse that had a price tag of $238 in Brazilian money, which was equal to $150 in American money. I kept trying to tell her "no" pushing it away, and she kept trying to give it to me, speaking in Portuguese, which is the native language . Finally Lynnie said, "She wants to give it to you. Just receive it." Wow! I had told Lynnie and Rita earlier that I was desiring a pink blouse! That's favor!

Releasing injustices releases favor with God and releases Him to move wonderful ways, even reversing the situations. It's so simple to do. Declaring audibly the following is the best way I know to do it.

RELEASING INJUSTICE

1. I pluck out the seed of injustice that was planted in my heart when ....
   (Be specific and reach into your heart.)
2. I give it to You, Lord Jesus.(Lift it up to Him)
3. I release the injustice of .... in Jesus name! (Be specific)
4. I sever any legal contract I have made with the spirit of injustice, take authority over it and command it to go in Jesus name!
5. I proclaim the favor of God and favor with men and I proclaim greatness over my life!

CHAPTER SIXTEEN

FRESH BREAD

There is no fragrance in a house like the aroma of freshly baked bread from the oven. I'm not normally a big bread eater myself, but I could eat half a loaf when it's fresh from the oven! I can still remember smelling the bread in the oven when Mom would bake it, which she did nearly every week. I loved to eat it warm with butter and homemade strawberry jam.

Jesus is the Fresh Bread in my house. When I began studying this, I discovered that God was really into eating and I realized I inherited it from Him. He began in Genesis talking about what we should not eat. A disastrous thing for Adam and Eve, and for us, is to eat of the tree of knowledge of good and evil. Why is that? We all want to be smart, don't we? We were never intended to know good and evil. We are to eat from the tree of life, which is Jesus. He is our righteousness. When we eat of Him continually we'll know what we are to do and not do. We are not to judge by the flesh, but by the Spirit of God.

In Exodus 16, in the second month after they had left Egypt, all of the Israelites were in the wilderness. They were complaining against Moses and Aaron about not having food and drink, and wanting to go back to Egypt where there was plenty to eat.

Even though they were complaining against the Lord, He opened the doors of heaven and rained down manna on them to eat every morning, except the Sabbaths, for forty years. Every evening for forty years, except on the Sabbaths, He sent quail for them to eat. Every day they were to gather enough for that day, except for the sixth day, when they were to gather for the Sabbath as well as the day before the Sabbath. There was always enough! What an awesome faithful God!

> God says, "Because I have called and you refused, I have stretched out My hand and no one paid any attention, because you blew off my counsel and hated My correction, ...because they hated knowledge and didn't choose the fear of the Lord, they would have none of My counsel and despised My every rebuke, they shall eat the fruit of their own way." (Proverbs 1:24-31)

That does not sound tasty to me! I know that my own way would lead to destruction. The fruit would be pretty rotten! I don't want to eat that!

> Death and life are in the power of the tongue, and those who love it shall eat the fruit. (Proverbs 18:21)

What we are speaking is so important. There is power in those words to bring life or death. What we speak is what we will eat!

God gives an invitation.

> Ho! Everyone who thirsts, Come to the waters; And you who have no money, come, buy and eat. Yes, come buy wine

> *and milk without money and without price. Why do you spend money for what is not bread, and your wages for what does not satisfy? Listen carefully to me and eat what is good, and let your soul delight itself in abundance. Incline your ear and come to Me. Hear, and your soul shall live; And I will make an everlasting covenant with you – the sure mercies of David.* (Isaiah 55:1-3)

> Jesus said, *"My food is to do the will of Him who sent Me, and to finish His work."* (John 4:34)

He was saying that He gets His nourishment from doing the will of God. So it is with us. When I take time to hear what God is asking me to do, and I obey and do what God says, it gives me nourishment. My spirit is built up! I am strengthened and renewed! Fresh water is released and flowing through me and not polluted water that has just been setting dormant.

About five thousand men, along with women and children, had followed Jesus because they saw the signs that He did. Obviously they hadn't thought to bring lunch.

> *Jesus asked Philip, "Where are we going to buy bread for all these people to eat?" Jesus was testing him, as He knew what He was going to do. Philip answered, "Two hundred denarii worth of bread is not sufficient for them, that every one of them may have a little."* (John 6:7)

Andrew, whose ministry was to connect people, found a boy who had brought his lunch of five loaves of barley bread and two small fish. That doesn't seem like enough to us, but Jesus thought that was just the right amount because He took them, gave thanks, and distributed them to His disciples. The disciples then distributed them to the people, as much as they wanted. They all got filled up! He then told the disciples to gather up all the leftovers. The fragments of five barley loaves filled up twelve baskets!

The following day, people were seeking Jesus. Jesus told them they were seeking Him because they got filled up on the loaves. He was saying they missed the sign. He told them,

> *"Do not labor for the food which perishes, but for the food which endures to everlasting life, which the Son of Man will give you, because the Father has set His seal on Him."* (John 6:27)

We spend so much of our time and energy gaining things that will perish. He provides the food that gives life and lasts forever.

They wanted to know how they could work the works of God.

> *Jesus answered, "This is the work of God that you believe in Him whom He sent."* (John 6:29)

The definition of believe is to cleave to, trust, rely on, have faith in.

Most of us are so into striving, working, and performing. Jesus is waiting for us to press into Him and trust in and rely upon Him. Then just do what He says and we'll work the works of God and see miraculous results.

They wanted Him to perform for them.

> *"What sign will You perform then, that we may see it and believe You? What work will You do? Our fathers ate the manna in the desert."* (John 6:30)

> *Then Jesus said to them, "Most assuredly, I say to you, Moses did not give you the bread from heaven, but My Father*

gives you the true bread from heaven. For the bread of God is He who comes from heaven and gives life to the world." (John 6:32-33)

The fact that Jesus called Himself the True Bread indicates that there is false bread. There are a lot of things people look to for their nourishment. They all look enticing, but are a big deception. They are meant to seduce you into the way that leads to destruction. They become like eating stale bread, that looks bad, smells bad, and tastes bad.

Then they said to Him, "Lord, give us this bread always." And Jesus said to them, "I am the bread of life. He who comes to Me shall never hunger, and he who believes in Me shall never thirst." (John 6:34-35)

He is not talking about coming to Him one time and sitting in a pew once in a while or even every week. He's talking about continually coming to Him, eating and drinking of Him. He will satisfy our hunger and thirst. He's the only one who can.

"I assure you, most solemnly I tell you, he who believes in Me [who adheres to, trusts in, relies on, and has faith in Me] has (now possesses) eternal life. I am the Bread of Life [that gives life – the Living Bread]" (John 6:47-48 Amplified Bible)

And Jesus said to them, "I assure you, most solemnly I tell you, you cannot have any life in you unless you eat the flesh of the son of Man and drink His blood [unless you appropriate his life and the saving merit of His blood]. He who feeds on My flesh and drinks My blood has (possesses now) eternal life, and I will raise him up [from the dead] on the last day. For My flesh is true and genuine food, and My blood is true and genuine drink. He who feeds on My flesh and drinks My blood dwells continually in Me, and I [in like manner dwell continually] in him. Just as the living Father sent me and I live by (through, because of) the Father; even so whoever continues to feed on Me [whoever takes Me for his food and is nourished by me] shall [in His turn] live through and because of Me." (John 6:53-57 Amplified Bible)

If you want that fresh bread in your life, it's all about appropriating, to your own life, what Jesus offers you in His body (healing) and His blood (cleansing) and eating of Him and His presence on a continual basis. Jesus is our nourishment. He is our necessity for sustaining life.

So slide up to His table and eat until you're full. Drink in of His Holy Spirit until you are overflowing with His life.

CHAPTER SEVENTEEN

RAGS TO RICHES

Let's take a look at the closets and cupboards of the house. Suppose one closet is full of worn and torn rags. You feel like that's what you need to wear because you inherited them. You think that's probably what you deserve. However, your Dad lives just up the street and he has told you to come help yourself to anything you like. In his closet are fine robes fit for royalty. You don't avail yourself to that supply of robes because it just seems beyond your means to wear them. Your cupboards only contain beans and crackers, so that's what you have been living on. However, at Dad's house, there is a pantry stocked full of all kinds of food and a freezer full of the finest cuts of meat. You have been told to help yourself, but again, you feel it is beyond your means.

I relate this to a story about Mephibosheth. He was Jonathan's son. When he was five years old, his daddy Jonathan was killed in battle, along with his grandfather Saul. When his nurse heard about it, she grabbed him up and ran with him, out of fear, and she dropped him. From that point on, he was lame. He lived in fear and lack out in Lo Debar, which means "absence of God".

Some time later, King David was reigning over all Israel, and he administered judgment and justice to all his people. He remembered his covenant with Jonathan. Covenant is so powerful, because it is a contract that cannot be broken. Covenant is made out of love, not obligation. When Jonathan and David made a covenant, Jonathan took his royal robe off and put it on David. He gave him all of his armor, even his belt. When two people make a covenant, it's is an exchange. What's mine is yours and what's yours is mine.

Jonathan was dead. David asked if there was anyone still left of the house of Saul that he could bless for Jonathan's sake. Ziba, who had been Saul's servant, told him Jonathan had a son, who was lame in both feet, so David immediately sent for him.

Mephibosheth was gripped with fear, thinking the king may want to retaliate for all of Saul's cruel treatment of David. Mephibosheth came and fell on his face, bowing before David, and said, "Here is your servant."

> *David said, "Do not fear, for I will surely show you kindness for Jonathan your father's sake, and will restore to you all the land of Saul your grandfather, and you shall eat bread at my table continually."* (II Samuel 9:7)

Mephibosheth, bowing before David, said, "Who am I, your servant, that you should even look at me, a dead dog?" He saw himself as valueless, worthless, with no hope. He had resigned himself to living the rest of his life out in Lo Debar. He felt he deserved nothing better.

This is often the way we see ourselves. We see ourselves as of no value, worthless. Some of us have even been dropped. We see ourselves as unworthy and crippled emotionally, mentally, physically, or in other ways. God sought us out and made covenant with us by Jesus' blood in order to bless us, restore everything that has been taken from us, and to invite us to come eat at His table continually. Our covenant-keeping God invites us to come, restores us in every way, and invites us to slide right up to the table with the son of God, Jesus. We are no longer servants, but sons of the most high God! He invites us to eat continually at His table like the King's Son!

King David told Ziba, "I have given Mephibosheth all that belonged to Saul and to all his house. You and your sons and your servants will work the land for him and bring in the harvest for him, but Mephibosheth shall eat at my table always." Ziba had fifteen sons and twenty servants. Wow! Mephibosheth was willing to be a servant, as he saw himself as only a lowly servant, but suddenly he had thirty-six servants and, from this time on, he would eat at the king's table always! The power of a covenant is awesome! When David and Jonathan made covenant, it was an exchange. Everything they had belonged to each other!

Ziba agreed to do everything David asked. King David reiterated with,

"As for Mephibosheth, he shall eat at my table like one of the king's sons." (II Samuel 9:11)

Wow! This is such an awesome picture of how our Covenant-keeping God is with us! We come to Him feeling worthless, knowing we have no value outside of Him. We are all lame in some area of our lives, probably in all areas of our lives, physically, mentally, emotionally, and definitely spiritually. Oftentimes we can't even lift our heads up to look into His face. We come to Him, bowing before Him, willing to just be a servant of the Most High God. He looks at us with love, compassion, grace and favor. Immediately, He picks us up and welcomes us as a son of God! He invites us to slide up to the table and eat at the King's table, along with Jesus! He restores to us power, authority, and our inheritance! This story of David and Mephibosheth is a beautiful picture of what is spoken of in Romans 8:14-17.

> *For as many as are led by the Spirit of God, these are sons of God. For you did not receive the spirit of bondage again to fear, but you received the Spirit of adoption by whom we cry out, "Abba, Father." The Spirit himself bears witness with our spirit that we are children of God. And if children, then heirs – heirs of God and joint heirs with Christ, if indeed we suffer with Him, that we may also be glorified together.*

Again in Galatians 3:26 and 29 it is reiterated.

> *For you are all sons of God through faith in Christ Jesus. And if you are Christ's, then you are Abraham's seed, and heirs according to the promise.*

How awesome it is to be adopted by the God of the universe! One morning in 2003 I was studying about adoption in a hotel room in Laughlin, Nevada, while Jerry was working in that area. After a couple hours, I felt released of the Lord to leave. As I was leaving the room, I said, "Lord, thank you for my divine appointment today." I checked out and took my luggage to the car, and decided to go back into Colorado Belle and take advantage of the $1.99 breakfast. There was a long line and I don't like lines, but decided to wait anyway. Two older ladies got into line behind me. I could see they were part of a tour as they had name tags on. Both were named Jean. I asked the one directly behind me where she was from. She answered, "Melbourne, Florida", which was nearly 3000 miles away.

I said, "I was there once to a funeral." She responded, "You were?"

I continued, "Yes. My niece died of Lou Gehrig disease."

"Really? How old was she?" she asked.

"41"

"What was her name?' Jean asked.

"Robin Grice" I responded.

Jean began to shake and informed me, "I live in her apartment."

It was not just Robin's apartment building, but her very apartment! I had been in her apartment! We both began hugging each other and crying as we both recognized that this was indeed a divine appointment.

Then Jean said, "I never got to meet her, but I've certainly heard a lot about her from the neighbors. They all loved her."

We talked a little more and we were getting closer to the front of the line. I asked if the two ladies would like to join me for breakfast. I told them, I have never dined with a pair of Jeans before."

Jean said that she smoked. I don't like to eat with smoke blowing at the table, so I said I'd see them later. The Lord quickly asked me, "Kay, What are you doing?"

I quickly responded, "We'll have a table for three in smoking."

When we were seated Jean shared about taking care of her handicapped husband before he died a few months earlier. That's why she was in the handicapped apartment. She said she always prayed for strength to care for him, but would never think of asking for anything for herself. I began to share what the Lord had been showing me that morning about adoption.

The other Jean said, "I adopted my daughter after 10 years of barrenness. Then two years later, I gave birth to a son."

"Really?" I asked. "Tell me, did you love your daughter less than you loved your son?"

"Oh, no!" she declared. "Of course not!"

"When your family gathered at your table, did your daughter have to sit in a different place, like underneath, begging for crumbs, or was she given an equal place and portion with your son?"

"They were always given the same", she said.

"Well, what about at Christmas time, when you gave gifts. Did you give the son more than the daughter?"

"Heavens, no!" she responded.

I was then able to share with both of them about the Father God adopting us and giving to us as He gives to His Son.

I thought about my nephew Keith. My sister Anita and her husband Jim had four sons. Keith's mother lived just down the road. When she gave birth to Keith, she passed away right afterward. Anita began taking care of Keith and she and Jim loved him. After a while, they adopted him. They loved Keith just like they loved their other four sons. They finally got their little girl, which gave them a total of six children, equally loved.

When they ate their meals, Keith sat at the table with the rest. He didn't crawl around under the table eating the crumbs. When gifts were handed out at Christmas, he received equally. He didn't reject his gifts, saying, "I can't receive them. I'm adopted." He tore into the packages just like all the rest!

Keith did nothing to deserve his adoption. It was because of grace – undeserved favor. He just received the privileges of being a son.

We are all heirs of God and joint heirs with Christ! We need to receive the inheritance that has been given us! Receive the privileges of being a son.

> *But as many as received Him, to them He gave the right to become children of God, to those who believe in His name.* (John 1:12)

It's so amazing that our holy, almighty, awesome God says to us, "From now on you come as a son to My table and eat with

Me. It's not important where you have been or how you have seen yourself up to this point. Lay aside your fear and come to Me in faith. Believe what I have spoken to you. Come partner with My Son. Come eat at My table. Step up to the plate!" (Do you think that might be where that saying came from?)

CHAPTER EIGHTEEN

TENACITY (STICKING TO IT)

Tenacity is a vitally important ingredient for building a house God's way. It simply means "pressing through and sticking to it". It represents the glue, the nails, and the screws. How would the building components stick together without these? It would just fall apart. If you are going to be built, and your ministry is going to be built, the way God wants, tenacity is an absolutely necessary component. God is wanting to do something fresh and new, solid and durable. He is wanting to establish His kingdom on this earth and He is wanting to use you!

There are four stories in the Bible that give us an excellent picture of tenacity in operation. The first story is about four lepers.

Benahad, king of Syria, had gathered all of his army and had taken Samaria captive. The people couldn't go in or out of Samaria. Therefore, there was a great famine in the land. They were living on donkey's head and dove droppings. A donkey's head was selling for over fifty dollars and a pint of dove droppings was selling for three dollars and twenty-five cents. Imagine the husband coming in from a hard day of work. "What's for dinner, honey?" he asks. His wife answers, "I've scraped together all the money I could and I made you dove poop soup." Yummy, huh?

At the height of this great famine, Elisha the prophet gave a prophetic word of the Lord to the king that the famine would soon end and they would be able to buy a seah (eight gallons) of flour for sixty-four cents and 2 seahs (sixteen gallons) of barley for sixty-four cents. An officer that the king leaned on, who was filled with doubt and unbelief, responded accordingly, with doubt and unbelief.

> *He said, "Look, if the Lord would make windows in heaven, could this thing be?" Elisha responded, "In fact you shall see it with your eyes, but you shall not eat of it."* (II Kings 7:2)

When you receive a promise from the Lord and begin to claim it and expect it, there will always be those who will tell you, "No way! That will never happen!" We must be careful that we are not leaning upon the wrong people, those who are filled with doubt and unbelief.

Four lepers were sitting at the gate of Samaria, isolated from the rest of the people. There was no hope for lepers. They had an incurable disease, so they were totally rejected by the rest of their people and were not allowed to go into their own city. They were broke and looked like hopeless losers. They were sitting in the dirt begging for crumbs. Then the crumbs ran out. They had nothing to eat. They were starving.

Finally, the leprous men said to one another,

> *"Why are we sitting here until we die?"* (II Kings 7:3)

In other words, "What have we got to lose? The worst that can happen is that they'll kill us, but if we just sit here starving, we'll die anyway."

What came to my mind is Esther saying, *"If I perish, I perish!"* (Esther 4:16)

They rose up **at twilight**, not even in faith, but they rose up out of the dirt and started moving toward the enemy camp. They pushed beyond their comfort. It had to be very uncomfortable to have parts of their bodies rotting away. They pushed beyond their lack. They had no chariots, no horses, no means of transportation at all. They pushed beyond their weakness from not eating anything for some time. They pushed beyond the rejection and always feeling "less than". They pushed on, in spite of their circumstances! When they arrived at the outskirts of the camp, amazingly no one was there! There was no enemy there!

The Lord had caused the Syrian army to hear the noise of a great army of chariots and horses coming against them, and **at twilight**, they all fled the camp, leaving all of their belongings behind, even their horses and donkeys! At the very time that the lepers got up and began moving, the Lord caused the enemies to flee their camp!

What a revelation for us! If we'll get up and start moving in faith, God will go before us and clear the enemy camp! Don't be moved by what you think or what you've heard about the enemy or especially from the enemy. The enemy can't stand against the Lord! He can't stand against you when you move forward in the name and power of Jesus!

Those four lepers went on into the camp and entered a tent. They sat down in fine leather chairs. They stripped off their rags and put on designer clothes. They ate all the fine food they had longed for. They drank all that they wanted. They gathered fine clothes, as well as silver and gold; then went and hid them. They moved on to another tent and gathered everything from that one and went and hid them. Then suddenly they remembered their people, those who had rejected them. They decided they needed to share their knowledge with the king's people.

They returned to where they had hung out. They still couldn't enter Samaria, so they called out to the gatekeepers, "Hey, dude, we went into the enemy camp and there is no enemy there! The camp has been deserted by the enemy, and all their horses, donkeys, supplies, weapons, and treasures are still there! All of their tents are still intact!"

The gatekeepers called out to the king's household. Now the king, who had been leaning on that negative guy, responded in fear, doubt, and unbelief. He said, "It's only a trap of the enemy. When we go outside these walls, the enemy's going to attack us and take over the city." He had been hanging so long with that negative guy, he had become just like him. He would have stayed trapped in his lack and starvation, rather than step out in faith. But, thank God, he had a wise servant, who said, "Please, king, what do we have to lose? Why not take five of our remaining horses, load them up, and send them into the enemy camp to see if this report is true?"

So the king consented and sent two chariots loaded with men to go and check it out. As they went, they saw the road was full of garments and weapons, which the Syrians had thrown when they fled in a hurry. When they saw that, the messengers returned and told the king.

Then all the people went and gathered up, from the enemy camp, all that was left behind.

> *So it happened just as the man of God had spoken to the king, saying, "Two seahs of barley for a shekel and a seah of fine flour for a shekel, shall be sold tomorrow about this time in the gate of Samaria."* (II Kings 7:18)

The officer, upon whom the king had leaned, who had doubted the word of the Lord, was trampled to death at the gate by the people rushing to gather up the goods, Just as Elisha had spoken, that officer did not get to eat any of the plunder.

Many in the body of Christ have been sitting in the dirt, begging for crumbs. We've been in lack way too long. God is waiting for us to rise up and move forward in faith to do what he has called us to do.

We must stop believing the reports we hear on television about the economy. The economy is not our god. As we respond to our God, Jehovah Jireh, and move forward, the Lord will clear the way for us. The devil has no power against us as we move forward in faith and obedience. Let's rise up and move forward now!

Another great example of tenacity is this second story . It's of Zaccheus in Luke 19. He was rich, but he had always been very short, so he had felt deprived in that way. He had become a chief tax collector. That got him some recognition and feeling of self-worth. When he heard Jesus was in town, he desperately wanted a chance to see who Jesus was. People were swarming to the streets to see Him. He knew if he went out there, his chances of seeing him were almost zero. He was so short that all he had ever seen in a crowd were the backs of other people. His money couldn't buy him a front row seat. What could he do? He was determined to see Jesus.

Finally, in his desperation to see Jesus, he had an idea. He ran ahead to where Jesus was going and climbed up into a sycamore tree. That took some effort. First of all, to run fast was a feat for a really short guy. Secondly, to climb up into a tree was a challenging feat for him. It was his tenacity that pushed him beyond his comfort zone!

When Jesus came to that place, He looked up and saw Zaccheus. He actually looked up at him. He saw him! Not only that, He spoke to him and called him by name! Not only that, but He invited Himself to his house.

Jesus is attracted to desperate faith. He told Zaccheus to hurry and come down. He said, "I must stay at your house." Luke 19:5 He wasn't just going to pop in for a drink, He was going to stay at his house!

Zaccheus hurried and came down. He was quick to receive Jesus joyfully! He had an amazing encounter with Jesus!

Look at the response of "they."

> *"But when they saw it, they all complained, saying, 'He has gone to be a guest with a man who is a sinner.'* (Luke 19:7)

There will always be the "theys" who don't like what you are doing. People caught up in religion will not like it if you step out in faith and do what the Father says. Don't allow that to stop you. Aren't you glad Jesus wasn't controlled by the "theys" and "they alls"?

> *Zaccheus stood up and said to the Lord, "Look, Lord, I give half of my goods to the poor, and if I have taken anything from anyone by false accusation, I restore fourfold."* (Luke 19:8)

There was immediate evidence of his conversion. He brought forth fruit of his repentance. It was obvious to Jesus and everyone else that this guy Zaccheus was saved. His heart had been changed. His mind had been changed. His actions had been changed. His life had been changed because of His encounter with Jesus!

> *Jesus said, "Today salvation has come to this house. The reason I came is to seek and save that which was lost."* (Luke 19:9-10)

He had seen the hunger of Zaccheus and his tenacity to press through to see Him and He was drawn to him like a magnet!

The third story is of a woman who had a flow of blood for twelve years. According to the law, she was an outcast. She was rejected, lonely, and untouchable. She had spent all that she had on doctors and their remedies. No one could heal her. Now she was not only sick, but she was also broke. She was desperate. Then she heard about Jesus.

She said to herself, "If only I may touch his garment, I shall be made well." (Matthew 9:17)

That is desperate faith! She knew she would suffer severe consequences if she were caught touching anyone. Jesus was surrounded by masses of people. What a risk! She too had the mentality of Esther, "If I perish, I perish!"

This woman spoke her faith to herself, just as we need to do.

She crawled in from behind Jesus and touched the hem of his garment. Immediately the flow of blood stopped! Jesus responded at once and asked who had touched Him. The disciples asked, "With all these multitudes pressing around you and you ask, 'Who touched Me'?"

But Jesus said, "No man, Somebody really touched Me! I felt the power leave My body!" It was her desperate faith that drew from Him that power! It was her tenacity. It was her, "I'm gonna do this thing if it kills me."

She was busted. Her touch had not gone unnoticed. When the woman realized it, she fell down before Jesus, trembling for her life, and confessed that she had touched Him and was healed immediately.

Jesus said to her, "Daughter, be of good cheer; your faith has made you well. Go in peace." (Luke 8:48)

Jesus loves desperate faith, tenacious faith, and is quick to respond to it.

There was also Bartimaeus, the blind man who sat in the dirt begging. His legs worked, but he just sat, not knowing where to go. He heard a large crowd of people and he wondered what the commotion was all about. He was told that it was Jesus, so Bartimaeus cried out, "Jesus, Son of David, have mercy on me!"

> *Then many warned him to be quiet, but he cried out all the more, "Son of David, have mercy on me!"* (Mark 10:48)

There "they" are again, trying to suppress the voice of anyone wanting to move forward. He did not heed their order. He pushed through and cried louder and stronger. He got the attention of Jesus and it caused Him to stand still. He commanded the blind man to be called. Imagine that! Those who tried to shut him up now had to call the blind man to come forth to Jesus. They changed their tune really quickly and said to him in a whole different tone of voice,

> *"Be of good cheer. Rise, He is calling you."* (Mark 10:49)

Bartimaeus threw aside his garment and quickly rose and came to Jesus. He threw aside anything that would hinder him. That's what we need to do. If Jesus is calling us forth, we need to be quick to throw off everything that would hinder us in any way.

> *Jesus asked him, "What do you want Me to do for you?"* (Mark 10:51)

I believe that's what He is asking us today. "What do you want Me to do for you?" Think on that. What do you want? Speak it to the Lord. Bartimaeus told him he wanted to receive his sight.

Then Jesus said to him, "Go your way; your faith has made you well." And immediately he received his sight and followed Jesus on the road. (Mark 10:52)

Jesus responded to his desperate faith, his tenacious faith.

What is it you want from Jesus today? What is the desire in your heart? Go after it in tenacious faith. Believe the road will be cleared before you. Throw off every encumbrance. Follow Jesus on the road.

Allow me to use one more example of tenacious, the Apostle Paul. He had been beaten for preaching the gospel and had been bound up and put in prison. The Lord had come to him and stood by him and told him to be of good cheer, that he would also bear witness of Him in Rome.

More than forty Jews had banded together in a conspiracy that they wouldn't eat until they had Paul killed. They said, "Let's tell the commander to bring him down here for inquiry and when he gets here, we'll kill him." Paul's nephew heard of the proposed ambush and told Paul. Paul called for one of the centurions and told him to take the nephew to the commander and tell him about the conspiracy.

The commander sent for two centurions, told them to prepare two hundred soldiers, seventy horsemen and two hundred spear men to go to Ceasarea during the night and take Paul to Felix the governor.

Ananias the high priest came down, with other religious leaders, and accused Paul to the governor. They called him "a plague" and a "creator of dissension" and even accused him of trying to profane the temple.

Paul appealed to Caesar. He had the opportunity to go before King Agrippa. The whole assembly of Jews cried out that *"he was not fit to live any longer."* (Acts 25:24)

Then Agrippa said to Paul, "You are permitted to speak for yourself." After all that Paul had been through, look how Paul began.

"I think myself happy, King Agrippa." (Acts 26:2)

What an example to us! If Paul could think himself happy when all of his people were coming against him and wishing him dead, I believe we are able to think ourselves happy in whatever we encounter. That would be a good way to start every day, making a declaration, "I think myself happy."

Then Paul had the glorious opportunity to give his testimony to King Agrippa, and to say,

"Therefore, King Agrippa, I was not disobedient to the heavenly vision." (Acts 26:19)

I want to be able to say that. I want to be obedient to whatever God shows me to do. Paul went on to say he declared wherever he went that *they should repent, turn to God, and do works befitting repentance.* Acts 26:20

Paul shared Jesus, in his words, his actions, and his attitude, in such a powerful way that King Agrippa said,

"You almost persuade me to become a Christian." (Acts 26:28)

Paul certainly did his part, and wasn't responsible for the king's decision. The choice was up to the king, just as it is up to each of us. Paul was obedient to the heavenly vision, no matter what trials came his way. What an example he is of tenacity!

CHAPTER NINETEEN

FIGHT THE GOOD FIGHT

Suppose you are building a house and you get it half done and become weary and discouraged? Your arms, shoulders, and back are aching and you are tempted to quit. Even your hands hurt from hitting them, instead of the nail, with the hammer. (Missing the mark.) It's a great temptation to just give up and quit. Suddenly a vision of the completed dream house comes to mind and you know you have to keep going.

Over twenty years ago, I was struggling with something and I kept hearing the Lord say, "Fight the good fight!"

I knew that was in the Word, so I looked it up.

> *Fight the good fight of faith; lay hold on eternal life, to which you were also called and have confessed the good confession in the presence of many witnesses.* (1 Timothy 6:12)

I meditated on that for days and began to study it. According to Vine's Expository Dictionary, *Fight* means battle, contest, struggle, engage in a boxing bout. An intense struggle requires perseverance in loyalty to Christ and in contending with adversaries. *Perseverance* means to continue no matter what the opposition. An *adversary* is one who opposes or resists.

Remember the definition of faith, according to Hebrews 11:1:

> *Now faith is being sure of what we hope for, certain of what we do not see.*

Do you believe in what you don't see? Are you certain of it, even though you don't see it? If you are waiting to see before you believe, you may never see. We're talking about the faith that causes things to be made out of nothing you see! If you are only speaking about what you see, you may never see anything else! Visualize in your spirit what you believe God wants you to have.

Faith is believing what God says, no matter what I see, no matter what I hear, no matter what I feel! Jesus fought the good fight of faith, knowing what He would suffer for doing it. Paul and many others throughout the years, have fought the good fight of faith also.

You are to take hold of the eternal life to which you were called! Eternal life is not just the privilege of going to heaven someday.

> *And this is eternal life, that they may know You, the only true God and Jesus Christ, whom You have sent.* (John 17:3)

When you invited Jesus to live inside of you, He came in with all of His power, His ability, and His wisdom, as well as His love! The life of Jesus is inside of you and it's eternal! It began the day you invited Him in and dwells there for all of eternity! The word life is *zoe*, which means the life of God. That's rich, abundant, powerful life of God, the Holy Spirit-filled life! I'm pressing through all the resistance and I'm determined to take hold of that eternal life and hang on for all I'm worth. No one can take that life from me unless I let go, and I'm not letting go!

I was sitting in my office at McCulloch Corporation, where I was working in 1995. I was asking the Lord, "How do we fight the good fight?" His immediate response was, "Talk to a fighter."

Just then a man that had been a fighter walked into my office. What are the chances, huh? I asked him, "How do you fight a good fight?" He told me six things a fighter must do to fight a good fight.

1. **Know your trainer's voice.** When you're in the boxing ring, many voices are screaming from the sidelines, "Aim higher!" "Aim lower!" "Give up!" If you listen to any of those voices, you lose! You must build a relationship with your trainer. Our trainer is the Holy Spirit. You must spend time listening to Him, getting to know His voice. Jesus said,

"My sheep listen to My voice. I know them and they follow Me." (John 10:27)

   Declare that you won't entertain one thought from the devil or one word he has to say! Declare that you won't listen to any other voice that conflicts with the voice of the Holy Spirit.

2. **You need hard and lengthy training** to be toughened up and prepared for victory. You need to experience harder and harder challenges. God sent Moses to Pharaoh to bring the Israelites out of Egypt. Ten times Moses did exactly what God told him to do and

he got no results. He looked like a total failure. What if he had quit? The eleventh time that God gave him orders and he obeyed, God brought deliverance to a whole nation of people! I can relate to this one as for over forty years I've served God wholeheartedly, doing what I felt like He was saying when it wasn't popular, when it wasn't comfortable, and when it was lonely. Many times when I followed His instructions, I looked like a failure, but I was stretching my spiritual muscles. I know all of that training was in preparation for what I am doing now, and for what lies ahead for me. I'm getting excited even as I am writing this!

3. **Know your opponent!** Satan is not even a worthy opponent, but we must be discerning. We must ask God, "What is this coming against me or my loved ones?" Remember when David came up against Goliath, he asked, "Who is this coming against the armies of the living God?" He knew that he was in covenant with God and this attack was against the armies of the living God! We need to ask, "Holy Spirit, what is the source of this attack?" "What is the root?" We don't want to keep slapping away at the bad fruit without attacking the root. Know that the enemy wears masks and we must discern what is behind the mask. He works through flattery, lies, deceit, pride, gifts and talents, intimidation, manipulation, and control. God is a covenant-keeping God. What He says He will do. God is bound to His Word. He has the ability to bring it to pass.

4. **Know the precise strategy to defeat the enemy.** Listen to your trainer. He sees the bigger picture because of where he is located. He has the fight plan. You must follow that plan no matter what.

Each fight, (even with the same opponent) requires different strategy. You can't just do what has worked in the past. Remember Moses when twice he was in water crisis. The first time God told him to strike the rock. The second time God told him to speak to the rock. Both times Moses struck the rock and looked successful to the people. After all, he got water. But the second time, God was not pleased, and Moses missed out on entering the promised land. Invite and allow God to show you the truth, about you, about God, and about your enemy. God is so creative! He works in the opposite way of the enemy and natural man. Get God's perspective as He always sees the bigger picture.

5. **Position yourself to stay balanced and stay focused.** Your opponent aims at the middle for three reasons. A. To cause you to lose your breath, the life-flow. B. To cause you to lose your balance and fall. C. To cause you to forget who you are and what you have. Studying the Word of God and fellowshipping with other believers will keep you balanced and in the truth. Praying in your language and in the Spirit, praising, and worshiping God, listening to and obeying Him, will keep the life-flow going.

And having your feet shod in preparation (to face the enemy with the firm-footed stability, the promptness, and the readiness produced by the good news) of the Gospel of peace. (Ephesians 6:15)

As the fighter turned to go out the door of my office, he turned around and said, "Oh yeah, there's one more thing."

6. **Always keep your jockstrap in place.** Now that seems a little humorous, but immediately a scripture came to mind.

Stand therefore (hold your ground) having tightened the belt of truth around your loins. (Ephesians 6:14A)

The loins are the pro creative power, the reproductive part. The devil doesn't want you to reproduce. God wants you to reproduce! You are called to go and make disciples! Know the truth of who God is and who you are, made in the image of God! Know the truth of what God has called you to, your destiny! Know that He has equipped and empowered you to fulfill it! Know that nothing is impossible with God! Apply the truth daily!

Therefore gird up the loins of your mind. (I Peter 1:13)

Gird means to encircle, to clothe, to prepare, to brace, to surround (like a girdle).

Declare with me:

"I will fight the good fight of faith!"

"I will take hold of the eternal life of God to which I was called!"

"I accept the preparation necessary to step into my calling!"

CHAPTER TWENTY

LIGHTING THE WAY

A house would be really dark and dreary without light. You have to plan to fill the house with light or you won't even see the beauty of the house. There would be no life in the house if you had no light because life depends upon light. Just as the house is intended to have light, we are created to be filled with light. How do we get this house filled with light?

Upon what do you find your thoughts dwelling most of the time? Is it the darkness around you or is it the Light? As you look at the Light, I mean really focus on the Light, God will transpose from the Light, Who is Jesus, to you; then through you to the circumstances around you. The Light is powerful enough to transform them!

Just a few months after I had asked Jesus into my life and He transformed me with His love, His life, and His light, I was attending the weekly Bible Study at the parsonage of the Methodist Church. Val asked me to pray for her sister's granddaughter Hazel, who was in a mental hospital. I had never met Hazel. She was suffering from severe depression and was not even able to feed herself or respond in any way.

The next morning she was to be committed to an institution. I felt a powerful anointing as I began to pray that the light and life of Jesus Christ would go to her room and into Hazel, transforming her and setting her free! It was a short and simple prayer, spoken in faith. A couple weeks later I received a thank you card from Hazel, thanking me for the prayer. She had been instantly healed the evening of the prayer! The next morning as she had gone before a judge, he could see nothing wrong with her and even offered her a job! She was working at that job and singing in the church choir by the time she wrote the card!

In Him was life, and the life was the light of men. (John 1:4)

In Jesus is *zoe*: life as God has it, as He gave to Jesus, and He gives to us, as we become partakers through faith in Jesus Christ. That life is the light of men. As we allow Jesus to live freely in us and through us, He is the Light for all mankind.

That was the true Light which gives light to every man coming into the world. (John 1:9)

Jesus gives light to every man coming into the world. No man is without excuse, according to this verse. Obviously, He shows Himself to every person in some way.

Light is a luminous emanation, probably of force, from certain bodies, which enables the eye to discern form and color. Light requires an organ adapted for its reception. When the eye is absent, light is useless. Natural man is incapable of receiving spiritual light as he lacks the capacity for spiritual things. Believers are called "sons of light", because when they are born again, they receive the spiritual capacity for light and revelation.

But as many as received Him, to them He gave the right to become children of God, to those who believe in His name; who were born, not of blood, nor of the will of the flesh, nor of the will of man, but of God. (John 1:12,13)

We often hear people say, "We're all children of God." According to God's Word, only those who receive Jesus, who become born again of the Spirit, are truly children of God. Receive means to take to oneself, to accept for yourself. When you receive Jesus, you receive the light, the way, the truth, the life, the door, and so much more!

And of His fullness we have all received, and grace for grace. (John 1:16)

What is He full of? Grace and truth and all the fruit of the Spirit; love, peace, joy, kindness, goodness, patience, faithfulness, gentleness, self-control. He is full of the power of God!

Into each one of us who personally invites and receives Jesus into his heart and life, God comes, through Jesus, with all of His power and all of His provision, as well as His grace and His truth!

Grace means undeserved favor. He gives us one grace after another, heaping grace upon us. Grace bestows pleasure, delight and beauty! When we receive Jesus, we look different! We begin to receive His beauty! We feel different! We begin to feel His pleasure with us and His delight in us!

For weeks I have been impressed with this verse:

For the Lord takes pleasure in His people; He will beautify the humble with salvation. (Psalm 149:4,5)

I'm trying to get my head wrapped around the truth that God actually takes pleasure in me! He is making me beautiful!

When I saw myself as His Bride in a dream in 1993, I looked beautiful! I was glowing! It was so far beyond how I had ever seen myself that it amazed me! I'm just beginning to understand what I saw! Jesus began in me a beautification process the day I invited Him into my heart and life. As I allow Him to change and rearrange and work His Word into me, the beautification process progressively works in me until He makes me a Bride without spot or wrinkle. For a long time, I've felt that the spots were from actions or attitudes and sins we have committed. The wrinkles are from wrong responses to what others have done to us; those things we need to be healed from and set free of. This is a life-long process. We need to continually submit to the process, so we can be filled with His ever-increasing light and beauty!

Why is this so important?

The King will greatly desire your beauty; because He is your Lord, worship Him. (Psalm 45:11)

That tells me it is important to Jesus that we are beautiful! He desires it! He provides the beauty as we focus on Him and become more like Him. Worshiping Him as Lord enhances that beauty and we reflect His beauty.

Let the beauty of the Lord our God be upon us. (Psalm 90:17)

Jesus is preparing a Bride for Himself. He will not be unequally yoked. He will not have a Bride who is depressed, oppressed, or wounded. He won't have a Bride who is selfish, envious, halfhearted, or defeated. He won't have a Bride who is competing with herself, attacking herself, or judging herself. She will not be compromising in her walk. Jesus will have a holy, beautiful Bride who has made herself ready and submitted herself to the Holy Spirit's cleansing and preparations. She will be filled with His unconditional love. She will be filled with fervent love for her Bridegroom! She will be walking in power & authority! She will walk in wisdom and in truth. She will be full of peace and joy! The beauty of our God will be seen through her!

> *He gave me beauty for ashes, the oil of joy for mourning, the garment of praise for the spirit of heaviness that we may be trees of righteousness, the planting of the Lord, that He may be glorified.* (Isaiah 61:3)

He gives me beauty for ashes. God wants me to give Him my ashes. What are ashes? According to Webster, *ash* symbolizes grief, repentance, and humiliation. There are many things in life that I have felt grieved about; a lot of losses, foolish mistakes, wrong choices, some of which led to real messes. I have felt humiliated a number of times by things I have done or said, or by what others have done or said about me. I try to quickly repent when my sin is made obvious to me. All of these ashes I gladly relinquish to the Lord. Most of us have questioned at some point, "How could I ever be useful to the Lord now?" Don't let fear or shame keep you hanging on to the ashes. As quickly as we release the ashes to Him, He begins working more of His beauty into our lives.

I've done a lot of personal ministry in inner healing. Many people are not even aware of the root issues that keep them bound up in life. As the Holy Spirit leads in the personal session, He knows how to expose and uproot things that most would think were insignificant. When He lovingly meets them there at that point of contact, and they allow Him to come and heal and set them free, instantly their countenance changes! They immediately feel lighter and look brighter! The more transparency they've allowed, the more the light shines and the more God's beauty can be seen!

Jesus said, "I am the light of the world. He who follows Me shall not walk in darkness, but have the light of life." (John 8:12)

The word follows here does not mean to trail along behind from a distance. The literal translation is "in union with, in likeness." Focusing on Jesus, you will become in union with Him, one with Him, and in His likeness. You also will become the light of life.

"You are the light of the world, a city that is set on a hill cannot be hidden." (Matthew 5:14)

As you become more and more transparent, the light of Jesus shines more and more clearly through you.

If you are hiding your light under a bushel, no one can see the light or find the light. The world is desperate for the light. They have been in darkness for so long, they don't even know where to look for the light. They don't even know they need to look for the light. Some have looked in religion. It wasn't there. Some have looked in programs. It wasn't there. Some have looked in church people. It wasn't there. It is only found in Jesus and in His people who are willing to be transparent enough to allow His light to shine. What does that mean?

Transparent: To show oneself, to show through. Free from pretense or deceit. Having the property of transmitting light.

We are called and recreated to transmit light. Transmit means to send or convey from one person or place to another. To cause to pass through, as light. The light passes through us to bring out the God-colors in others.

We are told to be transformed by the renewing of our minds.

Transform: To change in composition or structure. To change in character or condition. To change the outward form or appearance of. Metamorphose: as a caterpillar into a butterfly. As we change on the inside, it will show on the outside. We even look brand new!

As we become what we are called to be, transformed, and allow ourselves to be transparent, the light of Jesus is transmitted through us to those who are part of a very dark world. What a powerful light we have been given! We are empowered to release that light into others who have been living in darkness!

We're called to be that beautiful bride, filled with glorious light, ready to meet her Bridegroom!

One day we, the Bride of Christ, will actually become a city of glorious light!

Then I, John, saw the holy city, New Jerusalem, coming down out of heaven from God, prepared as a bride adorned for her husband. (Revelation 21:2)

"Come, I will show you the bride, the Lamb's wife." And he carried me away in the Spirit to a great and high mountain, and showed me the great city, the holy Jerusalem, descending out of heaven from God, having the glory of God. Her light was like a most precious stone, like a jasper stone, clear as crystal. (Revelation 21:9-11)

CHAPTER TWENTY-ONE

SEEING HIS GLORY

A house reflects the personality, the character, and the activity of the owner. As God is allowed to rebuild the house of the Lord, which is each one of us, we will reflect Him. We reflect the personality, the character, the activity, and the glory of our Father God, our Creator.

We are hearing reports from all over the world today that God's glory is appearing in visible manifestations, such as gold dust and jewels of various kinds. Some are questioning the validity of it all. They say, "We're to walk by faith, not by sight."

I've studied about the glory a number of times and have read the Bible several times in many different versions. I have never seen before what I am now seeing in God's Word! Why? Because it is the *kairos* time for seeing God's glory. God is wanting people to believe that He is real and that heaven is real. He wants us to step into the realm of the supernatural! He sent Jesus to eliminate the separation between heaven and earth.

Remember when Moses was in the presence of God? He went outside the camp, pitched a tent, and called it the tabernacle of meeting. He expected to meet with the Lord! The

Lord did not disappoint him. He showed up in a powerful way and the people saw the cloud standing at the tabernacle door! God promised His Presence would go with Moses. Moses was not satisfied with just His Presence. He wanted more! He was bold and asked for more. He said, *"Please, show me Your glory."* Exodus 33:15-33

God was gracious to him and showed him the glory and allowed him to see His back! Moses spent forty days and forty nights up on Mount Sinai with God. When he came down the mountain, his face shown so much that people were afraid to come near him! The glory was something you could see!

I will never forget when we had the church across Havasu Lake and we had to take the ferry boat across. It was around 120 degrees out in the midst of July. We had to wait for the boat to come and when it arrived, it was not the air-conditioned boat, but the old boat without air-conditioning, so we sat outside. When we got across to Havasu Landing, Tom and I walked up the hill to get the van, which was also very hot. We drove the van out to the church and walked into a very hot building that had no air on. It took a while to cool once we turned it on. By then I was soaking wet. My hair was all flattened and my makeup was running off my face.

Because it was so hot, only one person showed up for church that night. I did as always and preached like there was a thousand. When Tom and I got back to the boat dock, the boat had just left, so it was an hour wait for the next one. The only place to go to get out of the heat was the casino, so we went and sat on a bench in the lobby.

Suddenly a young woman got up from the gambling table and ran out to the lobby and fell down at my feet, asking, "What is that on you?"

I looked at her and asked, "What? Sweat? Dirt? Running makeup?"

She answered, "No, It's God! I need to turn back to Him!" She asked me to pray with her, so she could give her life back to Him! (That could only have been His glory!)

Both Tom and I were in awe at what God had done! We were very thankful that we had paid the price to make that trip! We learned that night that His glory shows up when we, in ourselves, are spent for Him!

In Numbers 14:21-24 the Lord says,

"But as truly as I live, all the earth shall be filled with the glory of the Lord."

We know that God truly lives! When He says, all the earth, He means all the earth! He goes on to say that all those men had seen His glory! It was actually visible to the eyes! There seems to be a tie between seeing His glory and responding to His voice and seeing the land of promise because those who had seen and didn't respond to His voice would not be seeing their land of promise. My conclusion is this: See His glory! Respond to His voice! See your land of promise!

In 1 Samuel the glory of the Lord had been in the temple, but through the sin and corruption of the priests, the glory left so gradually that no one even knew it left until Eli's daughter-in-law named her baby Ichabod, which means the glory of the Lord is departed. That's pretty sad when the glory leaves and no one even realizes it's gone.

In II Chronicles 5:11-14 all the priests who were present had sanctified themselves and didn't keep to their divisions. There's an important ingredient. All these divisions must be eliminated. When all the praise and worshipers were as one, to make one sound, declaring the goodness and mercy of God, the house of the Lord was filled with a cloud! The priests couldn't continue ministering because of the cloud, because the glory of the Lord filled the house of God!

After that Solomon prayed an awesome prayer, and fire came down from heaven, and consumed the burnt offering and the sacrifices and the glory of the Lord filled the temple! The priests couldn't even enter the house of the Lord, because the glory of the Lord had filled the Lord's house! All the children of Israel saw the fire come down, and the glory of the Lord fill the Lord's house. (II Chronicles 7:1-3) They all responded by bowing, worshiping and praising the Lord, and declaring His goodness and His mercy!

David prayed,

"So I have looked for You in the sanctuary, to see Your power and Your glory." (Psalm 63:2)

He expected to see the glory of the Lord in the sanctuary.

He also declared,

"The Lord will give grace and glory. No good thing will He withhold from those who walk uprightly." (Psalm 84:11)

This was his declaration and his expectation. His grace and His glory are good things He will not withhold from us!

Solomon confessed,

"The wise shall inherit glory." (Proverbs 3:35)

It sounds like glory is part of our inheritance if we are wise.

God said, "I have created you for My glory." (Isaiah 43:7)

This was a real eye-opener for me! I have been created for God's glory. It's His plan for His glory to be seen on me!

God created men and women to see and hear in the spiritual realm. Adam and Eve walked and talked with God in the garden. They were spiritually alive! We were not intended to live according to what we see in the natural and determine what is good and what is evil. That's why God told Adam to eat of any tree in the garden except the tree of knowledge of good and evil. He wanted them to walk in relationship with God, walking in His righteousness, allowing Him to determine what was right, not by using their head knowledge and deciding for themselves what was right.

As we know from Genesis 3, Eve was deceived and Adam and Eve ate of the wrong tree, and suddenly their natural eyesight was illuminated! They could now determine for themselves what was good and what was evil. They lost their spiritual eyesight and died spiritually.

Jesus redeemed us from that spiritual deadness and blindness. Jesus said,

Most assuredly, I say to you, unless one is born again, he cannot see the kingdom of God. (John 3:3)

That indicates that if you are born again, you can now see the kingdom of God. Hallelujah! Why do so many believers not yet see? Either they haven't been told that they can or else they don't believe they can. Jesus said,

"*You shall know the truth and the truth shall make you free.*" (John 8:32)

So they just need to be told and then activated!

The next passage confirms that the glory is something to be seen on us.

Arise, shine; for your light has come! And the glory of the Lord is risen upon you. For behold, the darkness shall cover the earth, and deep darkness the people; But the Lord will

arise over you and His glory will be seen upon you. (Isaiah 60:1, 2)

When God says glory will be seen on you, glory will be seen on you! That passage goes on to say unbelievers will come to that light, so, obviously even they will see that glory! Kings will come to the brightness of the glory on you! Family members will be drawn to it. Great favor and finances will be drawn to the glory on you! We shall become the City of the Lord! If that doesn't light your fire, your wood is definitely wet!

God promises:

And I will shake all nations, and they shall come to the Desire of All Nations, and I will fill this temple with glory, says the Lord of hosts. The silver is Mine, and the gold is Mine, says the Lord of hosts. The glory of this latter temple shall be greater than the former, says the Lord of hosts. (Haggai 2:7-9)

We are in the latter days. You are the temple of the Holy Spirit. He lives in you. You are not your own.

You were bought at a price; therefore glorify God in your body and in your spirit, which are God's. (1 Corinthians 6:19, 20)

We were bought by the blood of Jesus. What a price! He paid the price for us so that we would glorify God. We are to carry His glory in our bodies and in our spirits! This glory is going to be greater than the glory that shone on the face of Moses!

For the earth will be filled with the knowledge of the glory of the Lord, as the waters cover the sea. (Habakkuk 2:14)

The whole earth is going to know about the glory! My little granddaughter Jaden, who was a three-year-old at the time, was visiting with us at church one Sunday. After church, we were waiting for the Dream catcher, which was the casino's boat that transported us to and from church on the Chemehuevi Reservation. Jaden said she had to go to the bathroom, so I took her into the casino restroom. As she walked into the restroom, she spontaneously looked up, threw up her hands, and burst out singing at the top of her lungs, "The whole earth is filled with His glory!" I believe she was a prophetic voice that the Lord used to express His excitement about the whole earth being filled with His glory!

What is the definition of glory? Weightiness, that which is substantial or heavy; glory, honor, power, wealth, authority, magnificence, fame, dignity, riches and excellency. It's His visible splendor. It's God's magnificent presence! Wow! Come on, glory!

At Jesus' birth, a multitude of angels appeared to the shepherds, praising God and saying,

> "*Glory to God in the highest and on earth. Peace, goodwill toward men!*" (Luke 2:14)

That is not where you usually see the punctuation, but there was no punctuation originally. I believe the angels were proclaiming that the glory of God in heaven was brought to earth that night through the birth of Jesus! His glory always bring peace and goodwill to men!

> *And the Word became flesh and dwelt among us and we beheld His glory, the glory of the only begotten of the Father, full of grace and truth.* (John 1:14)

That's the Word of God confirming His glory came to earth through Jesus, and His glory can be seen! "Beheld" means "saw." Jesus carried the glory and released His glory wherever He went. The people saw His glory!

Jesus manifested His glory when He changed the water into wine. Those vessels which were normally filled with water, for religious and traditional purposes, were suddenly filled with new wine, representing the Holy Spirit! Why was that the first miracle? Because it shows us that, from the start of His ministry on earth, religion and tradition won't cut it. We need to replace that with the new wine of the Holy Spirit!

Jesus said,

> "*And the glory which You gave Me, I have given them, that they may be one just as We are one.*" (John 17:22)

The same glory that the Father gave Jesus, He has given to you and me! It's his manifest presence in us that will make us one as Jesus and the Father are one! It's not something we can work at by doing the right stuff or by not doing the wrong stuff. It's about spending time in His presence, drawing from Him the life and love of the Father. When each one of us is doing that, we will flow together in oneness, just as Jesus and the Father do. His glory will be seen in us!

Jesus was passionate about displaying the glory of God in the earth by doing the works of God , which God had given Him to do. He desired to show us the Father. He always left a favorable impression of His Father, so that we would desire to have a relationship with Him. So we should be cognizant of leaving a favorable impression of God wherever we go. We want to allow Him to shine through us in a way that others will desire Him.

I heard God say, "I am not a lame God. I am tired of being portrayed as a wimpy God, a lame God, a weak God. I am God of the whole universe! I am all powerful, almighty! Nothing is too hard for Me! I live in you! Rise up, believers! Be believers! Be expectant! Move forward and take the land I have given you! You have access by faith through grace, undeserved favor! You haven't earned it, but Jesus has earned it for you, in your place, through His ultimate sacrifice. Through Jesus, you can step into the grace of God and continue standing in His grace and rejoice in the expectation of the glory of God." We should expect God's glory to be seen in us and through us!

> *Through our Lord Jesus Christ, we have access by faith into this grace in which we stand, and rejoice in hope of the glory of God.* (Romans 5:2)

When your faith is tested and trials come, it's time to press into God. Be willing to die to the flesh, and allow His glory to work in you, as you keep your focus on God and what He is doing.

> *His glory shall be revealed in us! All of creation is earnestly expecting and eagerly waiting to see the sons of God be revealed!* (Romans 8:18,19)

How will we be revealed or distinguished as sons of God? By the glory revealed in us!

God desires to:

> *make known the riches of His glory on vessels of mercy* (that's us) *which He had prepared beforehand for glory.* (Romans 9:23)

We've been prepared for His glory! God wants to make known the riches of His glory on us!

The glory to be seen on us today is much more glorious than the glory seen on Moses' face that people could not even look at! In fact, the glory seen on Moses was, in comparison, *no glory*! The glory to be seen on us today *exceeds much more in glory*! (2 Corinthians 3:7-11)

We become like what we focus on. If we focus on Jesus and His glory, we become like Him, *transformed from glory to glory!* (2 Corinthians 3:18)

Every storm or challenge, if we allow, will work for us a far more exceeding and eternal weight of glory. The key is to not focus on the storm or challenge, but to focus on Jesus and heaven. Everything we can't see in the natural is more real than what we see in the natural, and those unseen things are eternal. That will not only carry us through the storm, but will allow more and more glory to be worked into us. (2 Corinthians 4:16-18)

When those fiery trials come, we are to rejoice that we are counted worthy to share in Christ's sufferings, so His glory will be revealed in us, and *the Spirit of glory rests upon us.* (1 Peter 4:12-14)

We are called to be partakers of His glory!

Jesus suffered *to bring many sons to glory*! (Hebrews 2:10)

God wills to make known what are the riches of the glory, which is:

Christ in you, the hope of glory. (Colossians 1:27)

Jesus Christ lives in you! It is not just His character. It is not just His works. Jesus Christ, in all of His power and His glory, lives in you! That's why we can expect His glory to be seen in us and work through us! He is my expectation of glory!

Paul prays:

> *that the Father of glory, may give to you the spirit of wisdom and revelation in the knowledge of Him, the eyes of your understanding being enlightened; that you may know what is the hope of His calling, what are the riches of the glory of His inheritance in the saints and what is the exceeding greatness of His power toward us who believe, according to the working of His mighty power, which He worked in Christ when He raised Him from the dead and seated Him at His right hand in the heavenly places.* (Ephesians 1:17-20)

Our Father is the Father of glory! We are His inheritance! He bought us with a great price! He expects to see us filled with His powerful glory!

Paul prays that the Father would grant us,

> *according to the riches of His glory, to be strengthened with might through His Spirit in the inner man.* (Ephesians 3:16)

How rich do you think His glory is? *According to* means to the exact degree as. So, He is saying that we can pray that, to the exact degree of glory He has, we may be *strengthened with might through His Spirit in our inner man*!

Christ, the Anointed, in me, is my hope of glory!

We are standing at the brink of the greatest move of God ever experienced! We must stand in faith and, as the Holy Spirit leads us, we must move forward in faith, expecting His glory to manifest in and through us!

We will be the house of the Lord, filled with His glory, shining for all to see! We will be the light of the world, His city on a hill that cannot be hidden!

www.ingramcontent.com/pod-product-compliance
Lightning Source LLC
Chambersburg PA
CBHW071911110526
44591CB00011B/1640